A

Spiritual Clearance

for

America

Spiritualizing the World, vol 8

A Spiritual

Clearance

for America

KIM MICHAELS

Copyright © 2019 Kim Michaels. All rights reserved. No part of this book may be used, reproduced, translated, electronically stored or transmitted by any means except by written permission from the publisher. A reviewer may quote brief passages in a review.

MORE TO LIFE PUBLISHING

www.morepublish.com

For foreign and translation rights,

contact info@ morepublish.com

ISBN: 978-87-93297-61-6

The information and insights in this book should not be considered as a form of therapy, advice, direction, diagnosis, and/or treatment of any kind. This information is not a substitute for medical, psychological, or other professional advice, counseling and care. All matters pertaining to your individual health should be supervised by a physician or appropriate health-care practitioner. No guarantee is made by the author or the publisher that the practices described in this book will yield successful results for anyone at any time. They are presented for informational purposes only, as the practice and proof rests with the individual.

For more information: *www.ascendedmasterlight.com and www.transcendencetoolbox.com*

CONTENTS

Introduction 7

1 | Rethinking American democracy is the will of God 11

2 | Invoking better decisions in America 23

3 | The dilemma for the modern man and modern nations 51

4 | Invoking an openness to new solutions 63

5 | Let the era of fiat money come to an end 97

6 | Invoking an end to the era of fiat money 107

7 | The true alchemy of acceleration 141

8 | Invoking the alchemy of acceleration 149

9 | The purpose of democracy is not affluence for all 173

10 | Invoking a new vision of the purpose of democracy 181

11 | Stand up to the elitist tendencies in government 201

12 | Invoking an end to the elitist tendencies in government 209

13 | The need to transcend representative democracy 233

14 | Invoking direct democracy 239

15 | The true alchemy of freedom 259

16 | Invoking the true alchemy of freedom 267

17 | What it takes to be a good President of the United States 297

18 | Invoking a higher vision of the presidency 309

19 | A golden age view of what it means to be President 333

20 | Invoking a Golden Age President 345

INTRODUCTION

This book belongs to the series *Spiritualizing the World*. The books in this series are given by the ascended masters as workbooks that provide the knowledge and practical tools we need in order to make a contribution to solving concrete world problems. This book contains the knowledge and the tools we need in order to perform a spiritual clearance for the United States, especially Washington, D.C. These books do not contain foundational knowledge about ascended masters and their teachings. In order to make the most efficient use of this book, you need to have a general knowledge of the following topics:

- You need to know who the ascended masters are, how they give their teachings and how you can make the best use of them on a personal and planetary level. You can find extensive teachings on this in the books: *How You Can Help Change the World* and *The Power of Self*.

- You need to know how the earth functions as a cosmic schoolroom. You need to know your own role and the authority you have as a spiritual being in embodiment. You need to know the role of the ascended masters and how only we who are in embodiment can give them the authority to use their unlimited power to affect change on earth. You can find more on these topics in the first book in this series: *How You Can Help Change the World*.

- You need to know how to use the practical tools given by the ascended masters. You can find more on this topic in: *How You Can Help Change the World* and on the website: *www.transcendencetoolbox.com*.

- You need to know about the existence and methods of the dark forces who are ultimately responsible for creating problems on earth. You can find foundational teachings on this in: *Cosmology of Evil*.

How to use this book

There is no one way of using the teachings and tools in this book. However, if you want to make a significant contribution to solving America's problems, it is suggested that you start by following this program:

- You read one of the chapters in the book completely in order to increase your understanding of the topic.

- You give the invocation associated with that chapter once a day for nine days while studying the same chapter again.

The reasoning behind this program is that the chapters in the book form a progression. As you give an invocation for one chapter, you are also clearing your own consciousness from certain energies and illusions. This makes it easier for you to absorb and apply the teachings from the next chapter.

You can, of course, also read the book all the way through and then select one or more invocation(s) that you give several times. It is always more powerful to give an invocation once a day for nine or 33 days.

Giving the invocations in Washington, D.C.

The dictations in this book were originally given at significant locations in the Washington, D.C. area. In order to perform a more efficient clearance, it is a good idea to have a picture of the location (such as the Lincoln Memorial or the White House) to look at while you give the invocation.

If you have the opportunity, you can, of course, also travel to these locations and give the invocations there. It will, naturally, be more efficient if a group did this and gave the invocations together. It should be possible to visit all of the locations (possibly with the exception of Mount Vernon) in one day and give the invocations. The effect of an invocation is greatly multiplied by the number of people giving it at the same time. Obviously, this multiplication can also be achieved if people agree to do the invocations on a specific time and then give them from their homes.

If you, as an individual or a group, do decide to give the invocations on location, please be aware that the rules for where you can assemble can change from time to time, depending on the threat level assessed by the government. Always follow the current rules and do not in any way provoke the authorities. It is most likely not appropriate to give an invocation inside the Rotunda of the Capitol building (unless you can get a specific permit), but it is equally efficient to give it outside the building. Likewise, it is advisable to keep a safe distance to the White House and the Federal Reserve building.

1 | RETHINKING AMERICAN DEMOCRACY IS THE WILL OF GOD

This dictation was given outside the Lincoln Memorial in Washington, D.C.

MORE I AM. Master MORE I AM, and I am present at this Lincoln Memorial in Washington, D.C. to anchor the Flame of the Will of God in and around this monument to a person, who had a considerable momentum on embodying and applying the will of God. This topic of the will of God is illustrated in many overt and subtle ways in the life of Abraham Lincoln, who understood that you cannot take a black-and-white view, but that you must be balanced, you must look at the nuances. For indeed, the will of God is not set in stone, cannot be defined by a certain scripture or even by a certain principle that is always applied in the same way.

The will of God must be applied through Christ discernment, through a vision of a higher goal, a higher principle, a higher union. Indeed, what Abraham Lincoln did see – before and especially during his presidency – was the absolute need to preserve the United States as one nation under God. It was imperative for the future of democracy and freedom in the world that the United States was not split up into two or more separate nations that, then, could have been set at war with each other. Not only for the profit of the international bankers, but indeed also to divide and therefore allow the communist forces to conquer and take away freedom on a worldwide scale.

This, then, was the great credit of Abraham Lincoln: He saw this need to preserve the Union. Yet he also saw the need to balance this with the individual rights of each human being: the right to liberty, the right to life, and the right, of course, to be so free that each person could pursue happiness as he or she saw fit, without violating the same rights for other people. This, then, is indeed the delicate balance that must be found, if America is to make a smooth transition into the Golden Age. There is no way that America can move from where it is now to the Golden Age without Christ discernment. As we have attempted to explain many times, Christ discernment is a balanced view, the Middle Way that is beyond the dualistic extremes—that always want to take any issue into one extreme or the other or into a no-man's land in the middle where no decisions can be made.

The need to make decisions

Lincoln, then, also understood the need to make certain decisions. Certainly, I can, as an ascended master today (even though I was not an ascended master back then), look back at the time of Abraham Lincoln today and see that some of the decisions he made were not necessarily the highest possible, seen from a timeless perspective. Nevertheless, they were the highest possible that he could make, given who he was, given his knowledge and psychology and given the conditions he faced.

This, of course, is exactly the situation I faced in my embodiment as Thomas More and in several other embodiments. You are in the physical octave, you are in the matter realm, the Mother realm. There are certain decisions that must be made based on the current conditions. If those conditions are not ideal, as they quite frankly rarely are, then you must make the best possible decision based on your knowledge, based on the conditions, based on who you are—meaning your personal psychology and your state of consciousness. No one can do any more; no one is asked to do any more. You are asked to make the best possible decision, then learn from it, and then transcend your level of consciousness.

Those who make decisions and then look back with regret or self-condemnation, or look back with denial and refuse to learn, simply will not grow. This, unfortunately, is also the reason the lifestream that was embodied as Abraham Lincoln, has not yet qualified for his ascension. He had the potential to have qualified for this by now. Again, there is an unwillingness to learn, an unwillingness to transcend that level of consciousness, a desire to justify certain decisions. Thus, a lifestream can be stuck for several embodiments without being willing to simply look at the facts, admit what could have been done better, learn from it, forgive oneself, forgive others and then move on.

It is, truly, a model of what has happened to the entire nation of the United States. The United States has a relatively short history compared to many other nations. Nevertheless, the United States also has a tendency to look at its own history with denial, not being willing to acknowledge the lessons that need to be learned and the state of consciousness that needs to be transcended. This is very obvious, if you walk from this Lincoln Memorial a short distance to one of the most visited war monuments in Washington, D.C., namely the Vietnam War Memorial.

The Vietnam War is still a stain on the national psyche, which the United States has not been willing to openly debate. They have not been willing to learn the lessons, to look at the lessons, to even consider that there are lessons to be learned. This, then, is a state of denial that is out of touch, again, with the will of God. For the will of God is *not* to hold you in some hell forever, as has now been projected into the collective consciousness for 2,000 years, almost, by the Christian religion—and before that by other religions.

The will of God is self-transcendence

The will of God is that you transcend yourself constantly, that you are never stuck for very long. Thus, it is not the will of God to point out your mistakes in a condemnatory manner where you are told that you are wrong and that you can never rectify yourself in the eyes of God. On the contrary, it is the will of God to point out that what you did was the expression of a certain state of consciousness. If the consequences are not the highest possible, then there is an obvious need to transcend that state of consciousness. Of course, you only transcend your state of consciousness by being willing to look at it and learn the lessons.

This is indeed the entire fallacy of the fallen consciousness: You can follow an outer path that will qualify you for entry into heaven, without you having to look at your own consciousness. It is the path that has been promoted by the false teachers of East and West, and is still being promoted by those false teachers, be it the Indian gurus of today – who are promoting themselves as being God on earth and that you will be saved by just following them blindly – or be it the western false gurus, who in many cases are also promoting an outer path or even promoting that there is no path, for there is no God.

Neither of these two can, of course, be correct. How can you qualify for salvation by blindly following a guru that you see as being outside yourself? You can follow a guru for a time, but the purpose of a true guru – a true *external* guru – is to put you into oneness with your *internal* guru, your higher self, your Presence, your I AM and your I Will Be Presence. So that you become the open door for that Presence, instead of sitting there with the mind, analyzing and thinking that you have to have a standard for what you will do or what the Presence can do through you. You first have to analyze whether the Presence lives up to this standard before you are willing to let the Presence act through you.

This, my beloved, is not the will of God, it is not the power of God. The will of God is not definable by an external standard. You will never follow the will of God by having an external standard that you compare every situation to, and then you think you can mechanically determine what is the will of God for you to do in that situation. You become one with the will of God by being the open door for the Presence so that it is the will of your I Will Be Presence that is free to express itself spontaneously through your lower being, without having to go through any filter that comes from the separate self and the fallen consciousness.

Emptying yourself for the will of God

This is to some degree what you see in Abraham Lincoln, although you also see that he too had a standard, and he too was affected by this fallen consciousness. Nevertheless, at critical moments he was willing to go into his closet, so to speak, to go into his heart and sincerely pray. He was willing to come to that point where he would say: "God, I do not know what to do in this situation, I do not know what is right—show me." Then, he was given an inner impulse, for which he often could give no outer justification, and he dared to act upon it.

This, then, was what, in a situation that was extremely difficult and far from ideal, enabled him to accomplish the overall goal that he had set for himself, namely the preservation of the Union. This, of course, was also why he was assassinated by those forces who had started the civil war, not because of slavery but precisely to split up and divide the Union that they might conquer it. When they could not do this through the Civil War – because President Lincoln was the one man who stood against them – they, of course, as has happened so often, took their wrath out against the one individual that they knew was the very keystone in the arch, the very cornerstone that prevented them from toppling the entire building.

Lincoln was assassinated. Unfortunately, President Lincoln, the lifestream that was President Lincoln, then made the decision that he had wasted his life by taking a stand that was not what he should have done. Even to this day, this lifestream looks back with some regret at this lifetime, almost regretting having taken the stand—even though at the time, he saw from within that this was the only viable solution, given the situation as it was.

Many of you that I am speaking to have in past lives faced equally difficult decisions and situations. Not that you have all been leaders of great nations or kings or emperors, but you have faced these moral and ethical dilemmas in your personal lives or even in certain positions in society. Many of you also look back with regret, even though you are not consciously aware of it. You will see that if you examine your psyche, you will find these deep inner regrets where you somehow think you have done something wrong, you are missing something, you have failed in some way. Therefore, you are not acceptable in the eyes of God.

This is precisely the kind of self-examination that is the opposite dualistic polarity to denial. Denial is where you refuse to look at yourself and refuse to transcend. The opposite is that you blame yourself, and therefore also put yourself in a situation where you cannot transcend the past, you cannot move on. As I have said: It is the will of God that you transcend, that you move on. There is nothing on earth that you cannot transcend. It is the will of God, it is the Law of God that there is nothing in the material universe that can serve as a prison for your free Spirit.

You have the capacity to transcend *everything!* How do you transcend? Well, as we have said many times, by the Conscious You realizing that it is pure awareness, that it is an open door. Therefore, there is no standard on this earth that can hold the Conscious You and that can prevent the Conscious You from being in oneness with the Presence and being the open door for the Presence. When you are the open door for the Presence, you have no need to lament about the past. You are focused on the present and being that open door, being that clear pane of glass in the present moment, in the present situation. Then, the Presence might act through you unhindered so that the stream of light and creativity from the Presence might flow without being stopped, without being filtered or misdirected.

Being reborn

This is indeed what it means to be flowing with the will of God. I can tell you that the Law of God is very simple: If you are not willing to voluntarily flow and transcend yourself, you will become subject to the second law of thermodynamics. This means, quite simply, that all the structures you have – be it the *external* structures in society or the *internal* structures in your own mind – will be broken down. They will burn, and everything will become as ashes. When all of the outer things, that the Conscious You is so identified with, have been burned by the fire, then the Conscious You – realizing it is truly none of these outer things; it is truly pure awareness – well, then the Conscious You will rise as the Phoenix Bird from the ashes. It will spread its wings and soar towards the sky. This is the Law. This is the will of God.

Self-transcendence is the mandate. It *will* happen, either through the breakdown of your structures, or it will happen through you voluntarily giving up and letting go of those structures. They either die as the result of the second law of thermodynamics – because they are split apart by their own internal contradictions – or they die because you let them die and no longer feed them your Light, your energy, your attention. This, my beloved, is the will of God. This is the dilemma that America as a nation faces right now. This is why I have decided to anchor this Flame of the Will of God and the discernment between what is truly the will of God and the will of man, as defined by the fallen consciousness and the separate self, the ego.

1 | Rethinking American democracy is the will of God

The need to rethink American democracy

Will America be willing to transcend itself, to transcend, in fact, the very ideals upon which it is founded, and to take them to a higher level where they are not so bound by a certain interpretation or by certain laws that they are not able to adapt it to the changing conditions? Is it really that difficult to see that when the Founding Fathers wrote the Declaration of Independence or the Constitution, or many of the initial laws and charters, they also acted based on the situation as it was back then, the level of consciousness that they had individually and the level of the collective consciousness?

This was a very long time ago. Much brown water has flowed through the Potomac River since this capital was founded. It is high time to part the waters of the muddy river and walk across to a new vision of America and its true potential in the modern age. This is the vision that you can have, but you cannot have it until you are willing to let go of the old. You cannot see the new vision, as long as you are looking through the filter of the old. You must take off the colored glasses, you must be willing to question your old images, your own mental images, your graven images of what this nation is, what democracy is and what it means to be a free democratic nation.

What is the most famous, the most quoted statement made by Abraham Lincoln? It is that of a government that is "*of* the people, *by* the people and *for* the people." This was the original vision. However, what has become of that vision is simple. You have a nation today that has a government that is *of* the elite, *by* the elite and *for* the elite.

The reason this has happened is that the people have been lulled to sleep, they have allowed themselves to be lulled to sleep by the thought that in a free nation, their liberties cannot be taken away. Yet they have been systematically eroded to the point where the elite is now so in control of every aspect of American society, especially the economy, that the people are enslaved through the almighty dollar and the taxes and the financial instruments that nobody understands, not even the people who are using them to enrich themselves and control the nation.

Thus, it is high time that the people wake up, that they take a stand, much like President Lincoln had to wake himself up and realize that his Presidency was not going to be a walk in the park, as they say. It was going to be a most excruciating and difficult period, more difficult than that faced by any other American President so far. But I can tell you that the current American President and the one that will be elected – whoever that might be in the next election – is likely to also face very difficult decisions.

Reflect on democracy

Indeed, there is a need to step back, to rethink, to look once again. I might suggest that the only way to proceed, to get this higher vision, is to take a cue from this Lincoln Memorial, which during the bigger time of the year has on its East side the long reflection pond filled with water. What is a reflection pond? Well, it *reflects,* my beloved. It is a mirror, is it not? So this reflection pond is a symbol. First of all, it is a symbol for the fact that the universe is the cosmic mirror and that what you send out will be reflected back to you. This applies equally to a nation as it applies to an individual.

1 | Rethinking American democracy is the will of God

The United States has sent out certain signals by allowing the power elite to rule this nation and involve it in a number of wars. Those things will come back, they will be reflected in the coming years. When you realize this, you realize that before the things you have sent out come back to you, it is very, very constructive to have transcended the state of consciousness that caused you to send out the signals in the first place. When you do, you will indeed mitigate what is coming back. You will open up for the mitigation of what is coming back, and you will, of course, also be able to respond to what is coming back in a higher way than you can when you are in the same state of consciousness that caused you to send the impulse into the cosmic mirror.

Nevertheless, the other lesson that can be learned from this reflection pond is that it reflects; the water reflects the sky above. This is the ancient, universal, alchemical action "As Above, so below." What is the will of God? It is that things in the material universe reflect the vision of the Spirit, the vision of the Elohim, the vision of the ascended masters, the vision of your own higher selves. It is that everything is as Above so below. The only way for America to transcend itself and navigate the coming years, is to be willing to reach for that higher vision and realize that something is out of sync here, that this nation is not living up to its own founding principles. Nor is it living up to the even higher vision that could be brought forth today if the people and those in leadership positions were willing to reach for it.

America has become too much of a closed circle. "One nation under God, indivisible with liberty and justice for all." Well, it is debatable whether the United States is currently one nation under God, for the United States in deeply divided between those who are promoting an agnostic or atheist worldview and those who are promoting a traditional Christian fundamentalist worldview, a worldview that has no reality, no connection, to the true teachings of Christ. Thus, this is one division that must be overcome.

Is there liberty for all people in the United States? Is there justice for all people in the United States? Again, there is not. Therefore, these are things that must be openly acknowledged and debated so that things can be rectified. Then, of course, the higher vision of American democracy that needs to also be brought forth and debated. This, I will, before I get too eager here, allow the other Chohans to expound upon, as they will give other addresses throughout this nations' capital. Thus, I will seal this release and seal this capital and this monument in the Flame of the Will of God. It is done!

2 | INVOKING BETTER DECISIONS IN AMERICA

In the name of the I AM THAT I AM, Jesus Christ, I use the authority that I have as a being in embodiment on earth to call upon Master MORE to reinforce my calls and use my chakras to project the statements in this invocation into the collective consciousness and awaken the decision makers of America to a spiritual foundation for making decisions. Awaken Americans to the reality that we are spiritual beings and that we can co-create a new future by working with the ascended masters. I especially call for …

[Make your own calls here.]

Part 1

1. Master MORE, I invoke the Flame of the Will of God that you have anchored at the Lincoln Memorial, and I call for it to awaken the decision-makers of America.

> O Hercules Blue, we're one with your will,
> all space in our beings with Blue Flame you fill,
> a beacon that radiates light to the earth,
> bringing about our planet's rebirth.
>
> **O Hercules Blue, all life you defend,**
> **giving us power to always transcend,**
> **in you the expansion of self has no end,**
> **as we in God's infinite spirals ascend.**

2. I invoke the momentum of Abraham Lincoln on embodying and applying the will of God, and I call for it to awaken the decision-makers of America.

> O Hercules Blue, your wisdom so great,
> within us a sense of knowing create,
> a new frame of reference we suddenly gain,
> for going beyond duality's pain.
>
> **O Hercules Blue, all life you defend,**
> **giving us power to always transcend,**
> **in you the expansion of self has no end,**
> **as we in God's infinite spirals ascend.**

2 | Invoking better decisions in America

3. I invoke the awakening of the decision-makers of America to the realization that we cannot take a black-and-white view, but that we must be balanced, we must look at the nuances.

> O Hercules Blue, we lovingly raise,
> our voices in giving God infinite praise,
> in feeling your flame, so clearly we see,
> transcending the self is the true alchemy.
>
> **O Hercules Blue, all life you defend,**
> **giving us power to always transcend,**
> **in you the expansion of self has no end,**
> **as we in God's infinite spirals ascend.**

4. I invoke the awakening of the decision-makers of America to the realization that the will of God is not set in stone and cannot always be applied in the same way.

> O Hercules Blue, all life now you heal,
> enveloping all in your Blue-flame Seal,
> we're grateful for playing a personal part,
> In God's infinitely intricate work of art.
>
> **O Hercules Blue, all life you defend,**
> **giving us power to always transcend,**
> **in you the expansion of self has no end,**
> **as we in God's infinite spirals ascend.**

5. I invoke the awakening of the decision-makers of America to the realization that the will of God must be applied through Christ discernment, through a vision of a higher goal, a higher principle, a higher union.

> O Hercules Blue, your Temple of Light,
> revealed to us all through our inner sight,
> your power allows us to forge on until,
> we pierce every veil and climb every hill.
>
> **O Hercules Blue, all life you defend,**
> **giving us power to always transcend,**
> **in you the expansion of self has no end,**
> **as we in God's infinite spirals ascend.**

6. I invoke the awakening of the decision-makers of America to the delicate balance of harmonizing the need to preserve the nation with the individual rights of each human being.

> O Hercules Blue, I pledge now my life,
> in helping this planet transcend human strife,
> duality's lies are pierced by your light,
> restoring the fullness of our inner sight.
>
> **O Hercules Blue, all life you defend,**
> **giving us power to always transcend,**
> **in you the expansion of self has no end,**
> **as we in God's infinite spirals ascend.**

7. I invoke the awakening of the decision-makers of America to the realization that America cannot move from where it is now to the Golden Age without Christ discernment.

> O Hercules Blue, we set all life free,
> from the subtlest lies of duality,
> the prince of this world no more has a bond,
> for with you we go completely beyond.

> **O Hercules Blue, all life you defend,**
> **giving us power to always transcend,**
> **in you the expansion of self has no end,**
> **as we in God's infinite spirals ascend.**

8. I invoke the awakening of the decision-makers of America to the realization that Christ discernment is a balanced view that is beyond the dualistic extremes.

> O Hercules Blue, in oneness with thee,
> we open our hearts to your reality,
> your electric-blue fire within us reveal,
> our innermost longing for all that is real.

> **O Hercules Blue, all life you defend,**
> **giving us power to always transcend,**
> **in you the expansion of self has no end,**
> **as we in God's infinite spirals ascend.**

9. I invoke the awakening of the decision-makers of America to the realization that on earth we never have ideal conditions for making decisions, so we must do the best we can based on the situation.

> O Hercules Blue, you fill every space,
> with infinite Power and infinite Grace,
> you embody the key to creativity,
> the will to transcend into Infinity.

> **O Hercules Blue, all life you defend,**
> **giving us power to always transcend,**
> **in you the expansion of self has no end,**
> **as we in God's infinite spirals ascend.**

Part 2

1. I invoke the awakening of the decision-makers of America to the realization that we must make the best possible decision, then learn from it, and then transcend our level of consciousness.

> O Hercules Blue, we're one with your will,
> all space in our beings with Blue Flame you fill,
> a beacon that radiates light to the earth,
> bringing about our planet's rebirth.
>
> **O Hercules Blue, all life you defend,**
> **giving us power to always transcend,**
> **in you the expansion of self has no end,**
> **as we in God's infinite spirals ascend.**

2. I invoke the awakening of the decision-makers of America to the realization that the United States has a tendency to look at its own history with denial, not being willing to acknowledge the lessons that need to be learned, and the state of consciousness that needs to be transcended.

> O Hercules Blue, your wisdom so great,
> within us a sense of knowing create,
> a new frame of reference we suddenly gain,
> for going beyond duality's pain.
>
> **O Hercules Blue, all life you defend,**
> **giving us power to always transcend,**
> **in you the expansion of self has no end,**
> **as we in God's infinite spirals ascend.**

3. I invoke the awakening of the decision-makers of America to the realization that we need to openly debate issues because it is not the will of God to hold us in some limitation forever.

> O Hercules Blue, we lovingly raise,
> our voices in giving God infinite praise,
> in feeling your flame, so clearly we see,
> transcending the self is the true alchemy.

> **O Hercules Blue, all life you defend,**
> **giving us power to always transcend,**
> **in you the expansion of self has no end,**
> **as we in God's infinite spirals ascend.**

4. I invoke the awakening of the decision-makers of America to the realization that the will of God is that we transcend ourselves constantly, that we are never stuck for very long.

> O Hercules Blue, all life now you heal,
> enveloping all in your Blue-flame Seal,
> we're grateful for playing a personal part,
> In God's infinitely intricate work of art.

> **O Hercules Blue, all life you defend,**
> **giving us power to always transcend,**
> **in you the expansion of self has no end,**
> **as we in God's infinite spirals ascend.**

5. I invoke the awakening of the decision-makers of America to the realization that it is not the will of God to point out our mistakes in a condemnatory manner, where we are told that we are wrong and that we can never rectify ourselves in the eyes of God.

> O Hercules Blue, your Temple of Light,
> revealed to us all through our inner sight,
> your power allows us to forge on until,
> we pierce every veil and climb every hill.
>
> **O Hercules Blue, all life you defend,
> giving us power to always transcend,
> in you the expansion of self has no end,
> as we in God's infinite spirals ascend.**

6. I invoke the awakening of the decision-makers of America to the realization that what we did was the expression of a certain state of consciousness. And if the consequences are not the highest possible, then there is an obvious need to transcend that state of consciousness.

> O Hercules Blue, I pledge now my life,
> in helping this planet transcend human strife,
> duality's lies are pierced by your light,
> restoring the fullness of our inner sight.
>
> **O Hercules Blue, all life you defend,
> giving us power to always transcend,
> in you the expansion of self has no end,
> as we in God's infinite spirals ascend.**

7. I invoke the awakening of the decision-makers of America to the realization that we only transcend our state of consciousness by being willing to look at it and learn the lessons.

2 | Invoking better decisions in America

O Hercules Blue, we set all life free,
from the subtlest lies of duality,
the prince of this world no more has a bond,
for with you we go completely beyond.

**O Hercules Blue, all life you defend,
giving us power to always transcend,
in you the expansion of self has no end,
as we in God's infinite spirals ascend.**

8. I invoke the awakening of the decision-makers of America to the realization that the outer path is entirely false because we will never qualify for entry into heaven without having to look at our own consciousness.

O Hercules Blue, in oneness with thee,
we open our hearts to your reality,
your electric-blue fire within us reveal,
our innermost longing for all that is real.

**O Hercules Blue, all life you defend,
giving us power to always transcend,
in you the expansion of self has no end,
as we in God's infinite spirals ascend.**

9. I invoke the awakening of the decision-makers of America to the realization that the will of God is not definable by an external standard.

O Hercules Blue, you fill every space,
with infinite Power and infinite Grace,
you embody the key to creativity,
the will to transcend into Infinity.

**O Hercules Blue, all life you defend,
giving us power to always transcend,
in you the expansion of self has no end,
as we in God's infinite spirals ascend.**

Part 3

1. I invoke the awakening of the decision-makers of America to the realization that we will never follow the will of God by having an external standard that we compare every situation to, and then we think we can mechanically determine what is the will of God for us in that situation.

Michael Archangel, in your flame so blue,
there is no more night, there is only you.
In oneness with you, we're filled with your light,
what glorious wonder, revealed to our sight.

**Michael Archangel, your Knowing so strong,
Michael Archangel, oh sweep us along.
Michael Archangel, we're singing your song,
Michael Archangel, with you we belong.**

2. I invoke the awakening of the decision-makers of America to the realization that we need to become an open door for a higher power, and we do this only by emptying ourselves of all outer standards.

Michael Archangel, protection you give,
within your blue shield, we ever shall live.
Sealed from all creatures, roaming the night,
we remain in your sphere, of electric blue light.

Michael Archangel, your Knowing so strong,
Michael Archangel, oh sweep us along.
Michael Archangel, we're singing your song,
Michael Archangel, with you we belong.

3. I invoke the awakening of the decision-makers of America to the realization that we need to empty ourselves so we can say: "God, I do not know what to do in this situation, I do not know what is right—show me."

Michael Archangel, what power you bring,
as millions of angels, praises will sing.
Consuming the demons, of doubt and of fear,
we know that your Presence, will always be near.

Michael Archangel, your Knowing so strong,
Michael Archangel, oh sweep us along.
Michael Archangel, we're singing your song,
Michael Archangel, with you we belong.

4. I invoke the awakening of the decision-makers of America to the realization that when we are given an inner impulse, for which we often can give no outer justification, we need to dare to act upon it.

Michael Archangel, God's will is your love,
you bring to us all, God's light from Above.
God's will is to see, all life taking flight,
transcendence of self, our most sacred right.

Michael Archangel, your Knowing so strong,
Michael Archangel, oh sweep us along.
Michael Archangel, we're singing your song,
Michael Archangel, with you we belong.

5. I invoke the awakening of the decision-makers of America to the realization that we have all faced these moral and ethical dilemmas in our personal lives or even in positions in society.

Michael Archangel, you are the best friend,
from all worldly dangers you do us defend,
the devil no match for your power of light,
and therefore our souls can freely take flight.

Michael Archangel, your Knowing so strong,
Michael Archangel, oh sweep us along.
Michael Archangel, we're singing your song,
Michael Archangel, with you we belong.

6. I invoke the awakening of the decision-makers of America to the realization that we have deep inner regrets where we think we have done something wrong, and therefore we are not acceptable in the eyes of God.

Michael Archangel, as children we play,
we're bringing the earth into a new day,
we raise it from all of the patterns so old,
our planet's life story is by us retold.

> **Michael Archangel, your Knowing so strong,**
> **Michael Archangel, oh sweep us along.**
> **Michael Archangel, we're singing your song,**
> **Michael Archangel, with you we belong.**

7. I invoke the awakening of the decision-makers of America to the realization that denial is where we refuse to look at ourselves and refuse to transcend. The opposite is that we blame ourselves, and therefore we cannot transcend the past, we cannot move on.

> Michael Archangel, God's power you show,
> that you are invincible, this we do know,
> you are undivided and thus can withstand,
> anything coming from serpentine band.

> **Michael Archangel, your Knowing so strong,**
> **Michael Archangel, oh sweep us along.**
> **Michael Archangel, we're singing your song,**
> **Michael Archangel, with you we belong.**

8. I invoke the awakening of the decision-makers of America to the realization that it is the will of God that we transcend, that we move on.

> Michael Archangel, come raise now the earth,
> giving her thus a complete rebirth,
> collective the mind that we do now raise,
> for this we do give our infinite praise.

**Michael Archangel, your Knowing so strong,
Michael Archangel, oh sweep us along.
Michael Archangel, we're singing your song,
Michael Archangel, with you we belong.**

9. I invoke the awakening of the decision-makers of America to the realization that there is nothing on earth that we cannot transcend. It is the will of God, it is the Law of God, that there is nothing in the material universe that can serve as a prison for our free Spirit.

Michael Archangel, the earth is now new,
covered in Blue-flame as the morning dew,
our planet now sparkles throughout all of space,
as we are receiving your infinite Grace.

**Michael Archangel, your Knowing so strong,
Michael Archangel, oh sweep us along.
Michael Archangel, we're singing your song,
Michael Archangel, with you we belong.**

Part 4

1. I invoke the awakening of the decision-makers of America to the realization that we transcend by realizing that we are more than the outer identities, that there is a higher part of our beings.

2 | Invoking better decisions in America

> Michael Archangel, in your flame so blue,
> there is no more night, there is only you.
> In oneness with you, we're filled with your light,
> what glorious wonder, revealed to our sight.
>
> **Michael Archangel, your Knowing so strong,**
> **Michael Archangel, oh sweep us along.**
> **Michael Archangel, we're singing your song,**
> **Michael Archangel, with you we belong.**

2. I invoke the awakening of the decision-makers of America to the realization that we can become an open door for our higher beings, as President Lincoln was at times such an open door.

> Michael Archangel, protection you give,
> within your blue shield, we ever shall live.
> Sealed from all creatures, roaming the night,
> we remain in your sphere, of electric blue light.
>
> **Michael Archangel, your Knowing so strong,**
> **Michael Archangel, oh sweep us along.**
> **Michael Archangel, we're singing your song,**
> **Michael Archangel, with you we belong.**

3. I invoke the awakening of the decision-makers of America to the realization that the Law of God says that if we are not willing to voluntarily flow and transcend ourselves, the external structures in society or the internal structures in our own minds will be broken down.

Michael Archangel, what power you bring,
as millions of angels, praises will sing.
Consuming the demons, of doubt and of fear,
we know that your Presence, will always be near.

Michael Archangel, your Knowing so strong,
Michael Archangel, oh sweep us along.
Michael Archangel, we're singing your song,
Michael Archangel, with you we belong.

4. I invoke the awakening of the decision-makers of America to the realization that self-transcendence is the mandate. It will happen either through the breakdown of our structures, or it will happen through us voluntarily giving up and letting go of those structures.

Michael Archangel, God's will is your love,
you bring to us all, God's light from Above.
God's will is to see, all life taking flight,
transcendence of self, our most sacred right.

Michael Archangel, your Knowing so strong,
Michael Archangel, oh sweep us along.
Michael Archangel, we're singing your song,
Michael Archangel, with you we belong.

5. I invoke the awakening of the decision-makers of America to the realization that the dilemma that America faces is whether to let go of the old structures and embrace the new opportunities.

Michael Archangel, you are the best friend,
from all worldly dangers you do us defend,
the devil no match for your power of light,
and therefore our souls can freely take flight.

**Michael Archangel, your Knowing so strong,
Michael Archangel, oh sweep us along.
Michael Archangel, we're singing your song,
Michael Archangel, with you we belong.**

6. Master MORE, I invoke on behalf of the decision-makers in America your Flame of the Will of God and the discernment between what is truly the will of God and the will of man, as defined by the lower consciousness and the ego.

Michael Archangel, as children we play,
we're bringing the earth into a new day,
we raise it from all of the patterns so old,
our planet's life story is by us retold.

**Michael Archangel, your Knowing so strong,
Michael Archangel, oh sweep us along.
Michael Archangel, we're singing your song,
Michael Archangel, with you we belong.**

7. I invoke the awakening of the decision-makers of America to the realization that America must be willing to transcend itself, to transcend the very ideals upon which it is founded, and to take them to a higher level.

> Michael Archangel, God's power you show,
> that you are invincible, this we do know,
> you are undivided and thus can withstand,
> anything coming from serpentine band.
>
> **Michael Archangel, your Knowing so strong,**
> **Michael Archangel, oh sweep us along.**
> **Michael Archangel, we're singing your song,**
> **Michael Archangel, with you we belong.**

8. I invoke the awakening of the decision-makers of America to the realization that we cannot be so bound by interpretations or laws that we are not able to adapt to changing conditions.

> Michael Archangel, come raise now the earth,
> giving her thus a complete rebirth,
> collective the mind that we do now raise,
> for this we do give our infinite praise.
>
> **Michael Archangel, your Knowing so strong,**
> **Michael Archangel, oh sweep us along.**
> **Michael Archangel, we're singing your song,**
> **Michael Archangel, with you we belong.**

9. I invoke the awakening of the decision-makers of America to the realization that when the Founding Fathers wrote the Declaration of Independence or the Constitution, or many of the initial laws and charters, they acted based on the situation as it was back then, the level of consciousness that they had individually and the level of the collective consciousness.

> Michael Archangel, the earth is now new,
> covered in Blue-flame as the morning dew,
> our planet now sparkles throughout all of space,
> as we are receiving your infinite Grace.
>
> **Michael Archangel, your Knowing so strong,**
> **Michael Archangel, oh sweep us along.**
> **Michael Archangel, we're singing your song,**
> **Michael Archangel, with you we belong.**

Part 5

1. I invoke the awakening of the decision-makers of America to the realization that it is high time to part the waters of the muddy river and walk across to a new vision of America and its true potential in the modern age.

> Master MORE, come to the fore,
> we will absorb your flame of MORE.
> Master MORE, our will so strong,
> our power centers cleared by song.
>
> **Master MORE, your Sacred Heart,**
> **from this we will no more depart,**
> **we are forever in your flow,**
> **of Diamond Will that you bestow.**

2. I invoke the awakening of the decision-makers of America to the realization that we cannot have this new vision until we are willing to let go of the old. We cannot see the new vision as long as we are looking through the filter of the old.

Master MORE, your wisdom flows,
as our attunement ever grows.
Master MORE, we have a tie,
that helps us see through Serpent's lie.

**Master MORE, your Sacred Heart,
from this we will no more depart,
we are forever in your flow,
of Diamond Will that you bestow.**

3. I invoke the awakening of the decision-makers of America to the realization that we must take off the colored glasses, we must be willing to question our old images, our own mental images, our graven images of what this nation is, what democracy is and what it means to be a free democratic nation.

Master MORE, your love so pink,
there is no purer love, we think.
Master MORE, you set us free,
from all conditionality.

**Master MORE, your Sacred Heart,
from this we will no more depart,
we are forever in your flow,
of Diamond Will that you bestow.**

4. I invoke the awakening of the decision-makers of America to the realization that we no longer have a government that is "*of* the people, *by* the people and *for* the people." We have a government that is *of* the elite, *by* the elite and *for* the elite.

Master MORE, we will endure,
your discipline that makes us pure.
Master MORE, intentions true,
as we are always one with you.

Master MORE, your Sacred Heart,
from this we will no more depart,
we are forever in your flow,
of Diamond Will that you bestow.

5. I invoke the awakening of the decision-makers of America to the realization that this has happened because we have allowed ourselves to be lulled to sleep by the thought that in a free nation, our liberties cannot be taken away.

Master MORE, our vision raised,
the will of God is always praised.
Master MORE, creative will,
raising all life higher still.

Master MORE, your Sacred Heart,
from this we will no more depart,
we are forever in your flow,
of Diamond Will that you bestow.

6. I invoke the awakening of the decision-makers of America to the realization that our freedoms have been systematically eroded and the elite is now in control of every aspect of American society.

Master MORE, your peace is power,
the demons of war it will devour.
Master MORE, we serve all life,
our flames consuming war and strife.

**Master MORE, your Sacred Heart,
from this we will no more depart,
we are forever in your flow,
of Diamond Will that you bestow.**

7. I invoke the awakening of the decision-makers of America to the realization that the elite is now so in control of the economy that the people are enslaved through the almighty dollar and the taxes and the financial instruments that nobody understands, not even the people who are using them to enrich themselves and control the nation.

Master MORE, we are so free,
eternal bond from you we see.
Master MORE, we find rebirth,
in flow of your eternal mirth.

**Master MORE, your Sacred Heart,
from this we will no more depart,
we are forever in your flow,
of Diamond Will that you bestow.**

8. I invoke the awakening of the decision-makers of America to the realization that it is high time that the people wake up, that we take a stand, much like President Lincoln had to wake himself up and realize that his Presidency was not going to be easy.

Master MORE, you balance all,
the seven rays upon our call.
Master MORE, forever MORE,
we are the Spirit's open door.

**Master MORE, your Sacred Heart,
from this we will no more depart,
we are forever in your flow,
of Diamond Will that you bestow.**

9. I invoke the awakening of the decision-makers of America to the realization that the United States has sent out certain signals by allowing the power elite to rule this nation and involve it in a number of wars.

Master MORE, your Presence here,
filling up the inner sphere.
Life is now a sacred flow,
God Power we on all bestow.

**Master MORE, your Sacred Heart,
from this we will no more depart,
we are forever in your flow,
of Diamond Will that you bestow.**

Part 6

1. I invoke the awakening of the decision-makers of America to the realization that what America has sent out will come back, it will be reflected in the coming years.

Master MORE, come to the fore,
we will absorb your flame of MORE.
Master MORE, our will so strong,
our power centers cleared by song.

**Master MORE, your Sacred Heart,
from this we will no more depart,
we are forever in your flow,
of Diamond Will that you bestow.**

2. I invoke the awakening of the decision-makers of America to the realization that before the things we have sent out come back to us, it is constructive to have transcended the state of consciousness that caused us to send out the signals in the first place.

Master MORE, your wisdom flows,
as our attunement ever grows.
Master MORE, we have a tie,
that helps us see through Serpent's lie.

**Master MORE, your Sacred Heart,
from this we will no more depart,
we are forever in your flow,
of Diamond Will that you bestow.**

3. I invoke the awakening of the decision-makers of America to the realization that when we transcend the old consciousness, we will open up for the mitigation of what is coming back.

Master MORE, your love so pink,
there is no purer love, we think.
Master MORE, you set us free,
from all conditionality.

**Master MORE, your Sacred Heart,
from this we will no more depart,
we are forever in your flow,
of Diamond Will that you bestow.**

4. I invoke the awakening of the decision-makers of America to the realization that we will also be able to respond to what is coming back in a higher way than we can when we are in the same state of consciousness that caused us to send the impulse into the cosmic mirror.

Master MORE, we will endure,
your discipline that makes us pure.
Master MORE, intentions true,
as we are always one with you.

**Master MORE, your Sacred Heart,
from this we will no more depart,
we are forever in your flow,
of Diamond Will that you bestow.**

5. I invoke the awakening of the decision-makers of America to the realization that the only way for America to transcend itself and navigate the coming years, is to be willing to reach for a higher vision and realize that something is out of sync, that this nation is not living up to its own founding principles.

Master MORE, our vision raised,
the will of God is always praised.
Master MORE, creative will,
raising all life higher still.

**Master MORE, your Sacred Heart,
from this we will no more depart,
we are forever in your flow,
of Diamond Will that you bestow.**

6. I invoke the awakening of the decision-makers of America to the realization that America is not living up to the even higher vision that could be brought forth today, if the people and those in leadership positions were willing to reach for it.

Master MORE, your peace is power,
the demons of war it will devour.
Master MORE, we serve all life,
our flames consuming war and strife.

**Master MORE, your Sacred Heart,
from this we will no more depart,
we are forever in your flow,
of Diamond Will that you bestow.**

7. I invoke the awakening of the decision-makers of America to the realization that America has become too much of a closed circle. It is debatable whether the United States is currently one nation under God.

2 | Invoking better decisions in America

Master MORE, we are so free,
eternal bond from you we see.
Master MORE, we find rebirth,
in flow of your eternal mirth.

**Master MORE, your Sacred Heart,
from this we will no more depart,
we are forever in your flow,
of Diamond Will that you bestow.**

8. I invoke the awakening of the decision-makers of America to the realization that the United States in deeply divided between those who are promoting an atheist worldview and those who are promoting a traditional Christian worldview, which has no connection to the true teachings of Christ.

Master MORE, you balance all,
the seven rays upon our call.
Master MORE, forever MORE,
we are the Spirit's open door.

**Master MORE, your Sacred Heart,
from this we will no more depart,
we are forever in your flow,
of Diamond Will that you bestow.**

9. I invoke the awakening of the decision-makers of America to the realization that we don't have "liberty and justice for all" in the United States. These are things that must be openly acknowledged and debated so that things can be rectified.

Master MORE, your Presence here,
filling up the inner sphere.
Life is now a sacred flow,
God Power we on all bestow.

**Master MORE, your Sacred Heart,
from this we will no more depart,
we are forever in your flow,
of Diamond Will that you bestow.**

Sealing

In the name of the I AM THAT I AM, I accept that Archangel Michael, Astrea and Shiva form an impenetrable shield around myself and all constructive people, sealing us from all fear-based energies in all four octaves. I accept that the Light of God is consuming and transforming all fear-based energies that make up the dark forces working against America!

3 | THE DILEMMA FOR THE MODERN MAN AND MODERN NATIONS

This dictation was given at the Jefferson Memorial, Washington, D.C.

I AM Lanto, Chohan of the Second Ray. I am here to anchor a special flame of the Second Ray in and around this memorial, called the Jefferson Memorial, in Washington, D.C. Yet truly, from a spiritual perspective, it is not a memorial to one person. Of course, one of the problems seen in this United States is indeed the tendency to glorify, to almost deify, one person who has stood out from the crowd.

What is the true message that Christ came to bring to this earth? It is the potential of the individual to transcend any outer individuality, and simply be an open door for the true God-given individuality of the Presence. So that the I AM Presence can have an open door whereby it can flow through its omega aspect, the I Will Be Presence, into the material universe. Thereby, it can manifest the higher vision, the higher wisdom, rather than the false wisdom of the fallen beings based on the dualistic consciousness.

What you do indeed see here is that Thomas Jefferson represented precisely the dilemma of modern man. Will modern man deify the intellect, the reasoning mind, or will modern man be willing to recognize that there are limits to the intellect? There are limits to analysis, there are even limits to reason. One cannot look at the conditions in the material world – in the matter realm as it is right now – and use the analytical faculties of the intellect, or even the higher faculties of the reasoning mind, to extrapolate what is the higher vision of the Spirit.

The human dilemma

The fact is simple: Once conditions in the material realm have gone below the vision of the Spirit, you cannot go the other way through the intellect and the reasoning faculties because they can only look at what is known. Then, they can seek to extrapolate from there, but that will not get you back up to the higher vision once you have gone below it. This is the eternal human dilemma!

Once you have eaten the forbidden fruit – once you have started to define truth on your own, because you have set yourself, or rather the separate self, up as a god who can define, who can know, good and evil – well, then you are trapped in that dualistic reasoning. You can never go beyond it through the reasoning, through the intellect, through the separate self. You *cannot,* my beloved. It simply is not possible! It is indeed the wise ones who realize that it is not possible, and therefore accept the fact that there is a need to do something different, that we cannot continue to intellectualize, analyze and reason forever. Indeed, it will only get us so far, and we cannot go beyond a certain level. This is indeed the flame that I am here to anchor, as my messenger walks the periphery of the Jefferson monument, as I flow through the open door that he has provided.

The limitations of the intellect

Listen well, for indeed Thomas Jefferson exemplifies perfectly the person who had gone far with the intellect, gone far with the reasoning mind, who had a strong reasoning mind, a strong intellect and had developed it to a remarkable degree. Nevertheless, he also represents perfectly the limitations of this approach. You can go to a certain point, and then you simply cannot go higher. This is outpictured in the fact that Thomas Jefferson was the open door for bringing forth the Declaration of Independence, which says that all men are created equal without specifying any exceptions to this. Yet, Jefferson himself – in his gentleman's farm in Virginia – had his entire financial existence based on owning slaves.

This, then, illustrates the perfect dilemma that the intellect presents to man. It is so easy to see a higher principle, a higher truth, at the level of the mind. But it is an entirely different matter to carry it into physical manifestation through the emotions. Jefferson knew very well that slavery was not compatible with the Declaration of Independence. But when he came home to his beloved farm, high on that hill in Virginia, and when he sat there and looked out over this vast landscape, he knew also, through his reasoning mind, that there was no way for him to survive economically – given the times – without owning slaves. Thus, he was faced with a choice: Will you give up your convenient lifestyle in order to follow your higher vision, or will you cling to the familiar, cling to the convenient, in order to maintain that lifestyle?

Many have indeed faced this choice. All people on the spiritual path must and will face it. It is an initiation that no one can escape. For indeed, only those who have been willing to make the choice to forgo the convenient in order to follow a higher truth, only those can be the open door for this higher vision. Now, this is not to say that you all have to go out and do exactly what someone else has done with his life, for you each have a unique path to follow. You do not have to sell everything you have and stand there with nothing, for many of you are meant to serve in the positions you are in. There is nothing wrong with maintaining a lifestyle, as long as you do not let it control you and hold you back from taking the stand that you need to take.

Balanced wisdom

Do you see, it is not a matter – again – of taking the black-and-white approach that Master MORE talked about at the Lincoln Memorial? It is a matter of going towards the Middle Way, of knowing what is the higher truth, the higher vision for you, given your situation right now. It is not a matter of seeking some outer standard of wisdom, and then applying that to yourself in your own life, or seeking to apply it to the world—or seeking to fit yourself or the entire universe into a mental box created based on the fallen consciousness. Well my beloved, that is not the wisdom of the Second Ray, is it? How could it possibly be when indeed the reality is that the Second Ray is accelerated beyond the reach of the serpentine logic of

3 | The dilemma for the modern man and modern nations

the fallen consciousness? This, then, is what needs to happen right here in this nation's capital, if America is to navigate the stormy waters ahead. It is not a time to gather together a bunch of intellectuals who can sit there and come up with theories and models and statistics. It is indeed a time to gather together some who are willing to do what Abraham Lincoln did, go into their closet, into their hearts, and become completely empty of preconceived ideas, theories and models. Indeed, I can tell you that what the world will face, especially in the financial market but also in other areas of society in the coming years, can indeed not be dealt with based on any standard model.

There never has been any condition that compares to what the world will face, and therefore seeking to deal with these conditions based on previous models and previous experiences simply will not work. There will come a point where the only way to transcend the problems is to be completely open to a new vision, a new form of wisdom that is not based on reasoning from the past, reasoning from the existent. It is indeed based on imagining, being the open door to imagine, entirely new solutions that no one has thought of before.

This is to some degree what Thomas Jefferson was the open door for with the Declaration of Independence. But then, he could not continue it for the rest of his life. Thus, when he actually became President, and was faced with the practical realities of running a nation, he too often was not willing to do what Lincoln did and wrestle with the difficult decisions. Nor was he the decisive man of George Washington, and therefore he would tend to retreat from the problems, hoping that they would somehow solve themselves.

This, indeed, is another serious problem with the intellectual approach. If you are too intellectual, if you are too much in the mind, you tend to withdraw, you tend to avoid addressing problems openly. Thus, instead of dealing with the problems, you tend to deny and run away from them, hoping that they will somehow solve themselves. This, of course, is something you can indeed do at certain times. There are times where you can step back and where all you can do is to step back and wait for cycles to change. But there are also times where it is time to step forward and to deal with conditions openly. Again, there is not a black-and-white approach that I am advocating. I am advocating wisdom, attunement, where you cannot sit down and analyze: When should I step forward, when should I step back?

You must flow with the Spirit. Therefore, the only way to flow with the Spirit is to stop making decisions with the outer, intellectual, reasoning mind. This is not to say that you shut off the outer, reasoning mind. You do indeed need to use the reasoning faculties of your intellect and outer mind. But you do not use them in the sense that you analyze a problem and an issue, and then based on that analysis, you make a decision with the outer mind. You analyze the issue, and then – when you have come as far as you can with the intellect and the reasoning mind – you step back, you give up, you surrender your idea that you think you know it all, or the subtle sense imposed by the fallen beings that you *should* know it all.

You admit that you do not know. Then, you ask your higher self, your I Will Be Presence, to simply flow through you, as you are being the empty pane of glass, the open door. Therefore, you have no preconceived opinions of what should or should-not be. You allow the Spirit to flow. You allow the Spirit to blow where it listeth—and it will. Suddenly, things will open up. Suddenly, you will find that conditions will change and the right solution will manifest almost as if by magic. Why is this so?

Spiritual pride

It is so because men have the pride, the spiritual pride, of thinking they can accomplish something with the outer mind. What truly accomplishes something in this world, is the Light of the Spirit flowing through you. You may direct that Light, but it is the Light that is the doer. Once you become that clear pane of glass, that open door – who has no preconceived opinions, desires or expectations – well, then the Light will flow through you, and the Light will accomplish its work.

This is the true meaning of "One Nation Under God." One nation does not simply mean one nation that is not divided physically. It also means one that is not divided spiritually. Because the people have not fractured themselves into different factions, who all believe in their own pet theory about how the universe works and how America should be working. Instead, they have been willing to recognize that they do not know, that they do not see, and that they need a higher vision from beyond the intellect and beyond the conditions that are currently manifest in the matter realm. Matter will take on any form projected upon it by human beings. Matter has the potential to shake off that form, but it cannot do so by itself— except through the second law of thermodynamics that breaks down everything. Matter cannot accelerate itself beyond the present form, and this is why there is a need for those who will be the open doors for the Light that will flow and accelerate conditions beyond what is currently manifest.

There is no other way to change your individual life, there is no other way to change a nation, there is no other way to change a planet. It is only the Light that can do this. You, as human beings, can get yourselves *into* trouble, but if you think that you, yourselves as human beings, can also get yourselves *out of* trouble, then you are sorely mistaken. You will keep treading water until you acknowledge the fact that you need something from beyond the consciousness that precipitated current conditions.

That something is the wisdom and the vision, but it is also the Light itself. For only the Light has the power to change matter. What is matter? It is Light that has taken on a certain level of vibration. What can accelerate matter from that level is only Light of a higher vibration. This is the laws of physics that so many intellectual people – who believe science is the new religion – espouse. Yet, they are not willing to take it that one step further and recognize the reality that if everything is Light, then the Light that is manifest in the matter realm must have come from a higher form of Light, a higher form of energy and vibration. Thus, the only solution is, once again, to open up that flow from Above to below.

This can only happen, when there is a willingness to let go of one's preconceived images so that one is willing to let that which is below become, be transformed into, a reflection of what is Above. As Above, so below. There is no other way. This is the deeper reality that is indeed the one lesson that needs to be learned, not only by the United States of America but by all other nations.

The time to stand still is over

Secularism was a necessary step out of the quagmire of the false religion represented by the medieval Catholic church. As with everything else, secularism can only take you so far. Thus, there is now the need for the emergence of a universal form, a non-secular form, of spiritually to take the world higher from the present gridlock, the present treading water, if you will, that so many of the modern nations face.

What is indeed the purpose of having established a welfare state if you do nothing with it? If people spend their time and energy on empty entertainment, and therefore end up feeling like there is no purpose to their lives and thus even get into alcohol and drugs and other forms of escapism? There is only one point in establishing a welfare state, and that is to give more and more people free time so that they can spend their attention on the pursuit of a universal spiritual path that transcends any outer religions, but can be expressed through any outer religion, or no religion at all, as many organizations have already proven.

Thus, unless the industrialized nations can make this leap, as Thomas Jefferson was not able to make it, then the world will not stand still anymore. For the time to stand still is past, and therefore, it will be, as Master MORE said, a breakdown of the current order. This does not have the purpose, as some would think, to punish people for the sins of the past. It simply has one purpose only, and that is to break down the structures in the mind that are preventing people from becoming the open doors for a higher vision, for the imagination that is the open door for new ideas. If people are not willing to voluntarily question their ideas, then they must be broken down until they think there is nothing left. Then, finally, they are willing to be the open door and ask for some higher guidance.

Is it not so, my beloved, that many people have a tendency to ignore God when things are going well. Then, only when they are faced with a severe crisis, are they willing to look to the sky or look within and ask for help. As the old saying goes, there are no atheists in the foxholes. Does it not stand to reason that if people will not look into their own hearts while they are doing their daily business, then the second law of thermodynamics must precipitate some kind of situation that forces them into the foxholes. They, then, become willing to look beyond their mental images, their structures of the mind that are keeping them and their society and their nations and their planet trapped at a level that is long past, that should long ago have been transcended.

The dilemma of the United States

The United States in its current situation is very much like the older and retired Thomas Jefferson who sat there on his gentleman's farm in Virginia, looking out over the fields and the vast vistas, while his slaves were toiling in the fields. There is an elite in the United States of people in the government, people in the finance world, people in the media, people in industry and business, who are sitting there, thinking they have it all made materially, just as Thomas Jefferson thought.

They are not willing to acknowledge the simple fact that their wealth is built by the people who are slaving in their jobs, striving to raise their children—and this simply is not a sustainable situation. It cannot last. If the people will not stand up to the elite – and if the elite will not stand up for higher truth and transcend their privileged positions – well, then the system must collapse until there is, in people's vision, nothing left. Therefore, they are willing to open their minds and say: "Help us; show us a better way."

Stilling the mind

The moment that happens, the moment there is the openness, well, the call compels the answer. Ask and ye shall receive.

3 | The dilemma for the modern man and modern nations

When the student is ready, the teacher appears. What does it mean that the student is ready? Ah, so many ascended master students have completely misunderstood this concept. They think it means they have reached some advanced level of initiation. But it does not. It means, simply, that they have now finally become as the little children that Jesus said are of the Kingdom of God. They have opened their minds, they have unlocked their imagination; they have been willing to be the clear pane of glass, the open door. Then, the answer is immediately forthcoming.

Let go of your preconceived conditions, let go of your expectations. Still the mind. Still the mind. For do you not also see that there are many people who have been in crisis situations, and they have cried loudly for help from an external god in the sky without ever getting an answer? Yet those who have been able to find even a split second of complete silence, of complete openness, well, they always get an answer. This is proven over and over and over again by people who are spiritual and religious, by people who are not spiritual and religious. It is the openness of the mind that is the key to any kind of progress. It will not happen in any other way; it never *has,* it never *will.*

Do you not see even outpictured in Jesus' life, how he was greatly distraught in the Garden of Gethsemane the day before his crucifixion? Do you not see how he cried and sweated drops of blood in his agitation? Yet he found no rest, he found no peace, he found no answers. What, then, was the only way out? He was crucified, and hanging on the cross – feeling that everything was falling away from him, all of his structures in the mind were falling away – then, he finally found that moment of peace. He gave up the ghost, and then he was instantly delivered into a higher state of consciousness. This is the potential, not only for an individual but for an entire nation and for an entire planet. When there is the openness, the answer will be forthcoming. It cannot fail; it never has failed and it never will. The answer will be given when there is an open mind that can receive it. This is the law! Test it! Try it out! I dare you! Prove me herewith, sayeth the Lord, and I shall pour you out a blessing that there shall not be room to receive it!

Lanto I AM. My Flame is anchored for an indefinite period of time in and around this monument so that all who walk through it will feel it, and take with them a portion of the Light of the Second Ray. This will begin the alchemy that will transform them, until they see the limitations and the fallacy of their intellectual, reasoning minds—and thus become open to the direct guidance of the Spirit. This is the Flame that I have become one with, and that is why I earned the right to be the Chohan of the Second Ray. *That,* I AM. Lanto I AM.

4 | INVOKING AN OPENNESS TO NEW SOLUTIONS

In the name of the I AM THAT I AM, Jesus Christ, I use the authority that I have as a being in embodiment on earth to call upon Lanto to reinforce my calls and use my chakras to project the statements in this invocation into the collective consciousness and awaken the wise people of America to see new solutions to old problems. Awaken Americans to the reality that we are spiritual beings and that we can co-create a new future by working with the ascended masters. I especially call for …

[Make your own calls here.]

Part 1

1. Beloved Lanto, I invoke the special flame of the Second Ray that you have anchored in and around the Jefferson Memorial in Washington, D.C.

Beloved Apollo, with your second ray,
you open our eyes to see a new day,
We see through duality's lies and deceit,
transcending the mindset producing defeat.

**Beloved Apollo, thou Elohim Gold,
your radiant light our eyes now behold,
as pages of wisdom you gently unfold,
our planet is free from all that is old.**

2. I invoke the awakening of the wise people of America to the realization that one of the problems in the United States is the tendency to glorify, to almost deify, one person who has stood out from the crowd.

Beloved Apollo, in your flame we know,
that your living wisdom is always a flow,
in your light we see our own highest will,
immersed in the stream that never stands still.

**Beloved Apollo, thou Elohim Gold,
your radiant light our eyes now behold,
as pages of wisdom you gently unfold,
our planet is free from all that is old.**

3. I invoke the awakening of the wise people of America to the realization that the true message that Christ came to bring to this earth is the potential of the individual to transcend any outer individuality, and be an open door for the true God-given individuality of the Presence.

4 | Invoking an openness to new solutions

> Beloved Apollo, your light makes it clear,
> why we have taken embodiment here,
> exposing all lies causing the fall,
> you help us reclaim the oneness of all.
>
> **Beloved Apollo, thou Elohim Gold,**
> **your radiant light our eyes now behold,**
> **as pages of wisdom you gently unfold,**
> **our planet is free from all that is old.**

4. I invoke the awakening of the wise people of America to the realization that when the I AM Presence has an open door to the material universe, it can manifest the higher wisdom, rather than the false wisdom based on the dualistic consciousness.

> Beloved Apollo, exposing all lies,
> we hereby surrender all ego-based ties,
> we know our perception is truly the key,
> to transcending the serpentine duality.
>
> **Beloved Apollo, thou Elohim Gold,**
> **your radiant light our eyes now behold,**
> **as pages of wisdom you gently unfold,**
> **our planet is free from all that is old.**

5. I invoke the awakening of the wise people of America to the realization that Thomas Jefferson represented the dilemma of modern man. Will we deify the intellect or recognize that there are limits to the intellect?

Beloved Apollo, we heed now your call,
drawing us into Wisdom's Great Hall,
working to raise our own cosmic sphere,
together we form the tip of the spear.

**Beloved Apollo, thou Elohim Gold,
your radiant light our eyes now behold,
as pages of wisdom you gently unfold,
our planet is free from all that is old.**

6. I invoke the awakening of the wise people of America to the realization that there are limits to analysis, there are even limits to reason.

Beloved Apollo, your wisdom so clear,
in oneness with you, no serpent we fear,
the beam in our eye we willingly see,
we're free from the serpent's own duality.

**Beloved Apollo, thou Elohim Gold,
your radiant light our eyes now behold,
as pages of wisdom you gently unfold,
our planet is free from all that is old.**

7. I invoke the awakening of the wise people of America to the realization that we cannot look at the conditions in the material world as it is right now and use the analytical faculties of the intellect to extrapolate what is the higher vision of the Spirit.

Beloved Apollo, you help us to see
through your knowing eyes we truly are free,
we willingly stand in your piercing gaze,
empowered, we exit duality's maze.

> **Beloved Apollo, thou Elohim Gold,**
> **your radiant light our eyes now behold,**
> **as pages of wisdom you gently unfold,**
> **our planet is free from all that is old.**

8. I invoke the awakening of the wise people of America to the realization that once conditions in the material realm have gone below the vision of the Spirit, we cannot go the other way through the intellect and the reasoning faculties, because they can only look at what is known.

> Beloved Apollo, our vision we raise,
> we see that the earth is in a new phase,
> for nothing can stop the knowledge you bring,
> exposing that there's no separate thing.

> **Beloved Apollo, thou Elohim Gold,**
> **your radiant light our eyes now behold,**
> **as pages of wisdom you gently unfold,**
> **our planet is free from all that is old.**

9. I invoke the awakening of the wise people of America to the realization that when we seek to extrapolate from there, we will not get back up to the higher vision, once we have gone below it. This is the eternal human dilemma!

> Beloved Apollo, in wisdom's great mirth,
> we all are together uplifting the earth,
> as you now the true Flame of Wisdom reveal,
> all of earth's people can see what is real.

**Beloved Apollo, thou Elohim Gold,
your radiant light our eyes now behold,
as pages of wisdom you gently unfold,
our planet is free from all that is old.**

Part 2

1. I invoke the awakening of the wise people of America to the realization that once we have eaten the forbidden fruit, once we have started to define truth on our own, we are trapped in dualistic reasoning.

> Beloved Apollo, with your second ray,
> you open our eyes to see a new day,
> We see through duality's lies and deceit,
> transcending the mindset producing defeat.

**Beloved Apollo, thou Elohim Gold,
your radiant light our eyes now behold,
as pages of wisdom you gently unfold,
our planet is free from all that is old.**

2. I invoke the awakening of the wise people of America to the realization that once we have set ourselves, or rather the separate self, up as a god who can define good and evil, we can never go beyond it through the reasoning, through the intellect, through the separate self.

4 | Invoking an openness to new solutions

Beloved Apollo, in your flame we know,
that your living wisdom is always a flow,
in your light we see our own highest will,
immersed in the stream that never stands still.

**Beloved Apollo, thou Elohim Gold,
your radiant light our eyes now behold,
as pages of wisdom you gently unfold,
our planet is free from all that is old.**

3. I invoke the awakening of the wise people of America to the realization that it is not possible to use reason to go beyond reason, and therefore we need to do something different.

Beloved Apollo, your light makes it clear,
why we have taken embodiment here,
exposing all lies causing the fall,
you help us reclaim the oneness of all.

**Beloved Apollo, thou Elohim Gold,
your radiant light our eyes now behold,
as pages of wisdom you gently unfold,
our planet is free from all that is old.**

4. I invoke the awakening of the wise people of America to the realization that we cannot continue to intellectualize, analyze and reason forever. It will only get us so far, and we cannot go beyond a certain level.

Beloved Apollo, exposing all lies,
we hereby surrender all ego-based ties,
we know our perception is truly the key,
to transcending the serpentine duality.

> **Beloved Apollo, thou Elohim Gold,**
> **your radiant light our eyes now behold,**
> **as pages of wisdom you gently unfold,**
> **our planet is free from all that is old.**

5. I invoke the awakening of the wise people of America to the realization that Thomas Jefferson exemplifies the person who had a strong intellect and had developed it to a remarkable degree. He also represents that we can go to a certain point, and then we simply cannot go higher.

> Beloved Apollo, we heed now your call,
> drawing us into Wisdom's Great Hall,
> working to raise our own cosmic sphere,
> together we form the tip of the spear.

> **Beloved Apollo, thou Elohim Gold,**
> **your radiant light our eyes now behold,**
> **as pages of wisdom you gently unfold,**
> **our planet is free from all that is old.**

6. I invoke the awakening of the wise people of America to the realization that this is outpictured in the fact that Thomas Jefferson was the open door for bringing forth the Declaration of Independence, and yet, Jefferson himself had his entire financial existence based on owning slaves.

> Beloved Apollo, your wisdom so clear,
> in oneness with you, no serpent we fear,
> the beam in our eye we willingly see,
> we're free from the serpent's own duality.

> **Beloved Apollo, thou Elohim Gold,**
> **your radiant light our eyes now behold,**
> **as pages of wisdom you gently unfold,**
> **our planet is free from all that is old.**

7. I invoke the awakening of the wise people of America to the realization that this illustrates the dilemma that the intellect presents to us. It is so easy to see a higher principle at the level of the mind, but it is harder to carry it into physical manifestation through the emotions.

> Beloved Apollo, you help us to see
> through your knowing eyes we truly are free,
> we willingly stand in your piercing gaze,
> empowered, we exit duality's maze.

> **Beloved Apollo, thou Elohim Gold,**
> **your radiant light our eyes now behold,**
> **as pages of wisdom you gently unfold,**
> **our planet is free from all that is old.**

8. I invoke the awakening of the wise people of America to the realization that Jefferson was faced with a choice: Will you give up your convenient lifestyle in order to follow your higher vision, or will you cling to the familiar, cling to the convenient, in order to maintain that lifestyle?

> Beloved Apollo, our vision we raise,
> we see that the earth is in a new phase,
> for nothing can stop the knowledge you bring,
> exposing that there's no separate thing.

**Beloved Apollo, thou Elohim Gold,
your radiant light our eyes now behold,
as pages of wisdom you gently unfold,
our planet is free from all that is old.**

9. I invoke the awakening of the wise people of America to the realization that only those who are willing to forgo the convenient in order to follow a higher truth, can be the open door for a higher vision.

Beloved Apollo, in wisdom's great mirth,
we all are together uplifting the earth,
as you now the true Flame of Wisdom reveal,
all of earth's people can see what is real.

**Beloved Apollo, thou Elohim Gold,
your radiant light our eyes now behold,
as pages of wisdom you gently unfold,
our planet is free from all that is old.**

Part 3

1. I invoke the awakening of the wise people of America to the realization that we need to go toward the Middle Way, of knowing what is the higher truth, given our situation right now.

Jophiel Archangel, in wisdom's great light,
all serpentine lies exposed to our sight.
So subtle the lies that creep through the mind,
yet you are the greatest teacher we find.

4 | Invoking an openness to new solutions

> **Jophiel Archangel, exposing all lies,**
> **Jophiel Archangel, cutting all ties.**
> **Jophiel Archangel, clearing the skies,**
> **Jophiel Archangel, the mind truly flies.**

2. I invoke the awakening of the wise people of America to the realization that it is not a matter of seeking some outer standard of wisdom, and then applying that to ourselves or seeking to apply it to the world.

> Jophiel Archangel, your wisdom we hail,
> your sword cutting through duality's veil.
> As you show the way, we know what is real,
> from serpentine doubt, we instantly heal.

> **Jophiel Archangel, exposing all lies,**
> **Jophiel Archangel, cutting all ties.**
> **Jophiel Archangel, clearing the skies,**
> **Jophiel Archangel, the mind truly flies.**

3. I invoke the awakening of the wise people of America to the realization that it is not a matter of seeking to fit ourselves or the entire universe into a mental box created based on the fallen consciousness.

> Jophiel Archangel, your reality,
> the best antidote to duality.
> No lie can remain in your Presence so clear,
> with you on our side, no serpent we fear.

**Jophiel Archangel, exposing all lies,
Jophiel Archangel, cutting all ties.
Jophiel Archangel, clearing the skies,
Jophiel Archangel, the mind truly flies.**

4. I invoke the awakening of the wise people of America to the realization that the wisdom of the Second Ray is accelerated beyond the reach of the serpentine logic of the fallen consciousness.

Jophiel Archangel, God's mind is in me,
and through your clear light, its wisdom we see.
Divisions all vanish, as we see the One,
and truly, the wholeness of mind we have won.

**Jophiel Archangel, exposing all lies,
Jophiel Archangel, cutting all ties.
Jophiel Archangel, clearing the skies,
Jophiel Archangel, the mind truly flies.**

5. I invoke the awakening of the wise people of America to the realization that going beyond the serpentine logic is what needs to happen in this nation's capital, if America is to navigate the stormy waters ahead.

Jophiel Archangel, now show us the way,
that leads us beyond duality's fray,
we long to discern the truth and the lie,
so we the serpentine knots can untie.

4 | Invoking an openness to new solutions

> **Jophiel Archangel, exposing all lies,**
> **Jophiel Archangel, cutting all ties.**
> **Jophiel Archangel, clearing the skies,**
> **Jophiel Archangel, the mind truly flies.**

6. I invoke the awakening of the wise people of America to the realization that this is not a time to gather together a bunch of intellectuals, who can sit there and come up with theories and models and statistics.

> Jophiel Archangel, your Presence is here,
> and therefore our minds are perfectly clear,
> in wisdom's great fount we do take a bath,
> and now we withstand the devil's own wrath.

> **Jophiel Archangel, exposing all lies,**
> **Jophiel Archangel, cutting all ties.**
> **Jophiel Archangel, clearing the skies,**
> **Jophiel Archangel, the mind truly flies.**

7. I invoke the awakening of the wise people of America to the realization that it is time to gather together some who are willing to do what Abraham Lincoln did, go into their closet, into their hearts, and become completely empty of preconceived ideas, theories and models.

> Jophiel Archangel, it is your great task,
> to raise all mankind, if only we ask,
> so now on behalf of those who are blind,
> we ask for your help in wisdom to find.

> **Jophiel Archangel, exposing all lies,**
> **Jophiel Archangel, cutting all ties.**
> **Jophiel Archangel, clearing the skies,**
> **Jophiel Archangel, the mind truly flies.**

8. I invoke the awakening of the wise people of America to the realization that what the world will face, especially in the financial market but also in other areas of society in the coming years, cannot be dealt with based on any standard model.

> Jophiel Archangel, your Presence we hail,
> your Light cutting through the serpentine veil,
> the serpents can no longer people deceive,
> for all now your Flame of Wisdom receive.

> **Jophiel Archangel, exposing all lies,**
> **Jophiel Archangel, cutting all ties.**
> **Jophiel Archangel, clearing the skies,**
> **Jophiel Archangel, the mind truly flies.**

9. I invoke the awakening of the wise people of America to the realization that there never has been any condition that compares to what the world will face, and therefore seeking to deal with these conditions based on previous models and previous experiences simply will not work.

> Jophiel Archangel, where else can we go,
> when we long the highest wisdom to know?
> You share with us gladly all that you are,
> and now our vision goes ever so far.

**Jophiel Archangel, exposing all lies,
Jophiel Archangel, cutting all ties.
Jophiel Archangel, clearing the skies,
Jophiel Archangel, the mind truly flies.**

Part 4

1. I invoke the awakening of the wise people of America to the realization that the only way to transcend the problems is to be completely open to a new vision, a new form of wisdom, that is not based on reasoning from the past, reasoning from the existent. It is indeed based on imagining, being the open door to imagine entirely new solutions.

Jophiel Archangel, in wisdom's great light,
all serpentine lies exposed to our sight.
So subtle the lies that creep through the mind,
yet you are the greatest teacher we find.

**Jophiel Archangel, exposing all lies,
Jophiel Archangel, cutting all ties.
Jophiel Archangel, clearing the skies,
Jophiel Archangel, the mind truly flies.**

2. I invoke the awakening of the wise people of America to the realization that if people are too intellectual, are too much in the mind, they tend to withdraw, they tend to avoid addressing problems openly.

Jophiel Archangel, your wisdom we hail,
your sword cutting through duality's veil.
As you show the way, we know what is real,
from serpentine doubt, we instantly heal.

Jophiel Archangel, exposing all lies,
Jophiel Archangel, cutting all ties.
Jophiel Archangel, clearing the skies,
Jophiel Archangel, the mind truly flies.

3. I invoke the awakening of the wise people of America to the realization that instead of dealing with the problems, intellectuals tend to deny and run away from them, hoping that they will somehow solve themselves.

Jophiel Archangel, your reality,
the best antidote to duality.
No lie can remain in your Presence so clear,
with you on our side, no serpent we fear.

Jophiel Archangel, exposing all lies,
Jophiel Archangel, cutting all ties.
Jophiel Archangel, clearing the skies,
Jophiel Archangel, the mind truly flies.

4. I invoke the awakening of the wise people of America to the realization that there is a time to step back, and a time to step forward and deal with conditions openly. In order to know the difference, we must flow with the Spirit.

Jophiel Archangel, God's mind is in me,
and through your clear light, its wisdom we see.
Divisions all vanish, as we see the One,
and truly, the wholeness of mind we have won.

Jophiel Archangel, exposing all lies,
Jophiel Archangel, cutting all ties.
Jophiel Archangel, clearing the skies,
Jophiel Archangel, the mind truly flies.

5. I invoke the awakening of the wise people of America to the realization that the only way to flow with the Spirit is to stop making decisions with the outer, intellectual, reasoning mind.

Jophiel Archangel, now show us the way,
that leads us beyond duality's fray,
we long to discern the truth and the lie,
so we the serpentine knots can untie.

Jophiel Archangel, exposing all lies,
Jophiel Archangel, cutting all ties.
Jophiel Archangel, clearing the skies,
Jophiel Archangel, the mind truly flies.

6. I invoke the awakening of the wise people of America to the realization that we use the reasoning faculties in the sense that we analyze a problem, and when we have come as far as we can with the intellect, we step back.

Jophiel Archangel, your Presence is here,
and therefore our minds are perfectly clear,
in wisdom's great fount we do take a bath,
and now we withstand the devil's own wrath.

> **Jophiel Archangel, exposing all lies,**
> **Jophiel Archangel, cutting all ties.**
> **Jophiel Archangel, clearing the skies,**
> **Jophiel Archangel, the mind truly flies.**

7. I invoke the awakening of the wise people of America to the realization that we give up, we surrender our idea that we think we know it all, or the sense that we *should* know it all.

> Jophiel Archangel, it is your great task,
> to raise all mankind, if only we ask,
> so now on behalf of those who are blind,
> we ask for your help in wisdom to find.

> **Jophiel Archangel, exposing all lies,**
> **Jophiel Archangel, cutting all ties.**
> **Jophiel Archangel, clearing the skies,**
> **Jophiel Archangel, the mind truly flies.**

8. I invoke the awakening of the wise people of America to the realization that we admit that we do not know. We ask our higher selves to flow through us, as we are being the open door.

> Jophiel Archangel, your Presence we hail,
> your Light cutting through the serpentine veil,
> the serpents can no longer people deceive,
> for all now your Flame of Wisdom receive.

> **Jophiel Archangel, exposing all lies,**
> **Jophiel Archangel, cutting all ties.**
> **Jophiel Archangel, clearing the skies,**
> **Jophiel Archangel, the mind truly flies.**

4 | Invoking an openness to new solutions

9. I invoke the awakening of the wise people of America to the realization that we have no preconceived opinions of what *should* or *should not* be. We allow the Spirit to flow. Suddenly, conditions will change and the right solution will manifest almost as if by magic.

> Jophiel Archangel, where else can we go,
> when we long the highest wisdom to know?
> You share with us gladly all that you are,
> and now our vision goes ever so far.
>
> **Jophiel Archangel, exposing all lies,**
> **Jophiel Archangel, cutting all ties.**
> **Jophiel Archangel, clearing the skies,**
> **Jophiel Archangel, the mind truly flies.**

Part 5

1. I invoke the awakening of the wise people of America to the realization that it is spiritual pride to think we can accomplish something with the outer mind.

> Master Lanto, golden wise,
> expose in us the ego's lies.
> Master Lanto, will to be,
> we will to win our mastery.
>
> **Master Lanto, Wisdom's Fount,**
> **with blessings we can hardly count,**
> **you are for earth a shining light,**
> **your Golden Wisdom oh so bright.**

2. I invoke the awakening of the wise people of America to the realization that what truly accomplishes something in this world is the Light of the Spirit flowing through us. We may direct that Light, but it is the Light that is the doer.

> Master Lanto, balance all,
> for wisdom's balance we do call.
> Master Lanto, help us see,
> that balance is the Golden Key.
>
> **Master Lanto, Wisdom's Fount,**
> **with blessings we can hardly count,**
> **you are for earth a shining light,**
> **your Golden Wisdom oh so bright.**

3. I invoke the awakening of the wise people of America to the realization that once we become a clear pane of glass with no preconceived opinions, desires or expectations, the Light will flow through us and accomplish its work.

> Master Lanto, from Above,
> we call forth discerning love.
> Master Lanto, love's not blind,
> through love, God vision we do find.
>
> **Master Lanto, Wisdom's Fount,**
> **with blessings we can hardly count,**
> **you are for earth a shining light,**
> **your Golden Wisdom oh so bright.**

4. I invoke the awakening of the wise people of America to the realization that this is the true meaning of "One Nation under

4 | Invoking an openness to new solutions

God." One nation does not mean a nation that is not divided physically. It also means one that is not divided spirituality.

> Master Lanto, we are sure
> as Christic lamb intentions pure.
> Master Lanto, we'll transcend,
> acceleration is our truest friend.

> **Master Lanto, Wisdom's Fount,**
> **with blessings we can hardly count,**
> **you are for earth a shining light,**
> **your Golden Wisdom oh so bright.**

5. I invoke the awakening of the wise people of America to the realization that we have fractured ourselves into different factions with theories about how the universe works and how America *should* be working.

> Master Lanto, we are whole,
> no more division in the soul.
> Master Lanto, healing flame,
> all balance in your sacred name.

> **Master Lanto, Wisdom's Fount,**
> **with blessings we can hardly count,**
> **you are for earth a shining light,**
> **your Golden Wisdom oh so bright.**

6. I invoke the awakening of the wise people of America to the realization that we need to recognize that we do not know, and that we need a higher vision from beyond the intellect and beyond the conditions that are currently manifest in the matter realm.

Master Lanto, serve all life,
as we transcend all inner strife.
Master Lanto, peace you give,
to all who want to truly live.

**Master Lanto, Wisdom's Fount,
with blessings we can hardly count,
you are for earth a shining light,
your Golden Wisdom oh so bright.**

7. I invoke the awakening of the wise people of America to the realization that matter will take on any form projected upon it by human beings. Matter has the potential to shake off that form, but it cannot do so by itself.

Master Lanto, free to be,
in balanced creativity.
Master Lanto, we employ,
your balance as the key to joy.

**Master Lanto, Wisdom's Fount,
with blessings we can hardly count,
you are for earth a shining light,
your Golden Wisdom oh so bright.**

8. I invoke the awakening of the wise people of America to the realization that matter cannot accelerate itself beyond the present form. This is why we need to be the open doors for the Light that will flow and accelerate conditions beyond what is currently manifest.

4 | Invoking an openness to new solutions

> Master Lanto, balance all,
> the seven rays upon our call.
> Master Lanto, we take flight,
> the threefold flame a blazing light.
>
> **Master Lanto, Wisdom's Fount,**
> **with blessings we can hardly count,**
> **you are for earth a shining light,**
> **your Golden Wisdom oh so bright.**

9. I invoke the awakening of the wise people of America to the realization that only the Light can change a nation. We human beings can get ourselves *into* trouble, but we cannot get ourselves *out of* trouble.

> Lanto dear, your Presence here,
> filling up the inner sphere.
> Life is now a sacred flow,
> God Wisdom we on all bestow.
>
> **Master Lanto, Wisdom's Fount,**
> **with blessings we can hardly count,**
> **you are for earth a shining light,**
> **your Golden Wisdom oh so bright.**

Part 6

1. I invoke the awakening of the wise people of America to the realization that matter is light that has taken on a certain level of vibration. What can accelerate matter from that level is only light of a higher vibration.

> Master Lanto, golden wise,
> expose in us the ego's lies.
> Master Lanto, will to be,
> we will to win our mastery.
>
> **Master Lanto, Wisdom's Fount,**
> **with blessings we can hardly count,**
> **you are for earth a shining light,**
> **your Golden Wisdom oh so bright.**

2. I invoke the awakening of the wise people of America to the realization that since everything is light, then the light that is manifest in the matter realm must have come from a higher form of light, a higher form of energy and vibration.

> Master Lanto, balance all,
> for wisdom's balance we do call.
> Master Lanto, help us see,
> that balance is the Golden Key.
>
> **Master Lanto, Wisdom's Fount,**
> **with blessings we can hardly count,**
> **you are for earth a shining light,**
> **your Golden Wisdom oh so bright.**

3. I invoke the awakening of the wise people of America to the realization that the only solution is to open up that flow from Above to below. This can only happen when there is a willingness to let go of one's preconceived images, so that one is willing to let that which is below be transformed into a reflection of what is Above.

> Master Lanto, from Above,
> we call forth discerning love.
> Master Lanto, love's not blind,
> through love, God vision we do find.
>
> **Master Lanto, Wisdom's Fount,**
> **with blessings we can hardly count,**
> **you are for earth a shining light,**
> **your Golden Wisdom oh so bright.**

4. I invoke the awakening of the wise people of America to the realization that the key to progress is "As Above, so below." This is the one lesson that needs to be learned by the United States of America.

> Master Lanto, we are sure
> as Christic lamb intentions pure.
> Master Lanto, we'll transcend,
> acceleration is our truest friend.
>
> **Master Lanto, Wisdom's Fount,**
> **with blessings we can hardly count,**
> **you are for earth a shining light,**
> **your Golden Wisdom oh so bright.**

5. I invoke the awakening of the wise people of America to the realization that secularism was a necessary step out of the quagmire of the false religion represented by the medieval Catholic church. As with everything else, secularism can only take us so far.

Master Lanto, we are whole,
no more division in the soul.
Master Lanto, healing flame,
all balance in your sacred name.

**Master Lanto, Wisdom's Fount,
with blessings we can hardly count,
you are for earth a shining light,
your Golden Wisdom oh so bright.**

6. I invoke the awakening of the wise people of America to the realization that there is a need for the emergence of a universal form, a non-secular form, of spiritually, to take us higher from the present gridlock that so many of the modern nations face.

Master Lanto, serve all life,
as we transcend all inner strife.
Master Lanto, peace you give,
to all who want to truly live.

**Master Lanto, Wisdom's Fount,
with blessings we can hardly count,
you are for earth a shining light,
your Golden Wisdom oh so bright.**

7. I invoke the awakening of the wise people of America to the realization that there is no purpose of having established a welfare state if we do nothing with it.

Master Lanto, free to be,
in balanced creativity.
Master Lanto, we employ,
your balance as the key to joy.

> **Master Lanto, Wisdom's Fount,
> with blessings we can hardly count,
> you are for earth a shining light,
> your Golden Wisdom oh so bright.**

8. I invoke the awakening of the wise people of America to the realization that there is only one point in establishing a welfare state, and that is to give people free time so that they can spend their attention on the pursuit of a universal spiritual path that transcends any outer religions.

> Master Lanto, balance all,
> the seven rays upon our call.
> Master Lanto, we take flight,
> the threefold flame a blazing light.

> **Master Lanto, Wisdom's Fount,
> with blessings we can hardly count,
> you are for earth a shining light,
> your Golden Wisdom oh so bright.**

9. I invoke the awakening of the wise people of America to the realization that unless the industrialized nations can make this leap, then the world will not stand still anymore. For the time to stand still is past, and there will be a breakdown of the current order.

> Lanto dear, your Presence here,
> filling up the inner sphere.
> Life is now a sacred flow,
> God Wisdom we on all bestow.

**Master Lanto, Wisdom's Fount,
with blessings we can hardly count,
you are for earth a shining light,
your Golden Wisdom oh so bright.**

Part 7

1. I invoke the awakening of the wise people of America to the realization that this does not have the purpose to punish people, but to break down the structures in the mind that are preventing people from becoming the open doors for a higher vision.

> Master Lanto, golden wise,
> expose in us the ego's lies.
> Master Lanto, will to be,
> we will to win our mastery.

> **Master Lanto, Wisdom's Fount,
> with blessings we can hardly count,
> you are for earth a shining light,
> your Golden Wisdom oh so bright.**

2. I invoke the awakening of the wise people of America to the realization that if we are not willing to voluntarily question our ideas, then they must be broken down until we are willing to be the open door and ask for higher guidance.

4 | Invoking an openness to new solutions

> Master Lanto, balance all,
> for wisdom's balance we do call.
> Master Lanto, help us see,
> that balance is the Golden Key.
>
> **Master Lanto, Wisdom's Fount,**
> **with blessings we can hardly count,**
> **you are for earth a shining light,**
> **your Golden Wisdom oh so bright.**

3. I invoke the awakening of the wise people of America to the realization that many people have a tendency to ignore God when things are going well. Only when they are faced with a severe crisis, are they willing look within and ask for help.

> Master Lanto, from Above,
> we call forth discerning love.
> Master Lanto, love's not blind,
> through love, God vision we do find.
>
> **Master Lanto, Wisdom's Fount,**
> **with blessings we can hardly count,**
> **you are for earth a shining light,**
> **your Golden Wisdom oh so bright.**

4. I invoke the awakening of the wise people of America to the realization that we must be willing to look beyond our mental images, the structures of the mind that are keeping us and our society trapped at a level that is long past, that should long ago have been transcended.

Master Lanto, we are sure
as Christic lamb intentions pure.
Master Lanto, we'll transcend,
acceleration is our truest friend.

**Master Lanto, Wisdom's Fount,
with blessings we can hardly count,
you are for earth a shining light,
your Golden Wisdom oh so bright.**

5. I invoke the awakening of the wise people of America to the realization that there is an elite in the United States of people in the government, people in the finance world, people in the media, people in industry and business, who are thinking they have it all made materially.

Master Lanto, we are whole,
no more division in the soul.
Master Lanto, healing flame,
all balance in your sacred name.

**Master Lanto, Wisdom's Fount,
with blessings we can hardly count,
you are for earth a shining light,
your Golden Wisdom oh so bright.**

6. I invoke the awakening of the wise people of America to the realization that those in the elite are not willing to acknowledge the simple fact that their wealth is built by the people who are slaving in their jobs—and this is not a sustainable situation.

> Master Lanto, serve all life,
> as we transcend all inner strife.
> Master Lanto, peace you give,
> to all who want to truly live.
>
> **Master Lanto, Wisdom's Fount,**
> **with blessings we can hardly count,**
> **you are for earth a shining light,**
> **your Golden Wisdom oh so bright.**

7. I invoke the awakening of the wise people of America to the realization that if the people will not stand up to the elite – and if the elite will not stand up for higher truth and transcend their privileged positions – then the system must collapse, until we are willing to open our minds and say: "Help us; show us a better way."

> Master Lanto, free to be,
> in balanced creativity.
> Master Lanto, we employ,
> your balance as the key to joy.
>
> **Master Lanto, Wisdom's Fount,**
> **with blessings we can hardly count,**
> **you are for earth a shining light,**
> **your Golden Wisdom oh so bright.**

8. I invoke the awakening of the wise people of America to the realization that the moment there is the openness, the call compels the answer. We must open our minds, unlock our imagination and then, the answer is immediately forthcoming. An open mind is the key to progress.

Master Lanto, balance all,
the seven rays upon our call.
Master Lanto, we take flight,
the threefold flame a blazing light.

**Master Lanto, Wisdom's Fount,
with blessings we can hardly count,
you are for earth a shining light,
your Golden Wisdom oh so bright.**

9. Beloved Lanto, I invoke your Flame, anchored at the Jefferson Monument, to begin the alchemy that will transform people, until they see the limitations and the fallacy of their intellectual, reasoning minds—and thus become open to the direct guidance of the Spirit.

Lanto dear, your Presence here,
filling up the inner sphere.
Life is now a sacred flow,
God Wisdom we on all bestow.

**Master Lanto, Wisdom's Fount,
with blessings we can hardly count,
you are for earth a shining light,
your Golden Wisdom oh so bright.**

Sealing

In the name of the I AM THAT I AM, I accept that Archangel Michael, Astrea and Shiva form an impenetrable shield around myself and all constructive people, sealing us from all fear-based energies in all four octaves. I accept that the Light of God is consuming and transforming all fear-based energies that make up the dark forces working against America!

5 | LET THE ERA OF FIAT MONEY COME TO AN END

This dictation was given at the Federal Reserve Building in Washington, D.C.

Paul the Venetian is the name of the Being that you know as the Chohan of the Third Ray. Yet I come not alone, for this is a task that is beyond the level of the Chohan. Thus, I have enlisted the assistance of the Archangels and the Elohim of the Third Ray of God Love, and they come in the full intensity of God Love, which is indeed the Ruby Fire. I have also enlisted and received Sanat Kumara and Lady master Venus who will also anchor their Presence here, as we indeed shall endeavor to complete a task as this messenger walks the perimeter of this building, called the building of the Federal Reserve in Washington, D.C.

We will anchor here, and in other centers around this Capital that deal with the economy and the finances, the Ruby Fire that will serve as the dividing line, as the light of such intensity that it forces people to make the choice between life and death. Thus, we indeed say, as the Word has gone forth from ancient times: "Choose Life!" Choose the life that will get the economy flowing into the golden-age matrix that Saint Germain has prepared for this nation and the world. Yet before this can happen, these monolithic institutions that attempt to control the money system, must indeed either transform themselves into non-elitist institutions, or they must be allowed to fail.

Willingness to submit individuality to the system

You have all heard the saying "hidden in plain sight," and indeed here in the center of Washington, D.C. – on what is called the National Mall that houses the monuments and institutions of American democracy – here in this, what we might call sacred place, sits this building that houses the Federal Reserve system. Its architecture very similar to that of many government buildings, thus to give the impression that this is indeed part of the government that was charged by the ascended masters through Abraham Lincoln with being a government *of* the people, *by* the people and *for* the people.

Yet I assure you that within the walls of this building, there is very little willingness to be *of* the people, *by* the people and *for* the people. For how do you gain access to this building? How do you become one of the insiders in the Federal Reserve System? Well, you become so only if you have already demonstrated a willingness to submit your individuality to the system. You cannot be a strong individual and enter the banking system that is tied to the Federal Reserve System; it simply is not possible.

If you are not willing to submit to the system, to surrender your individuality in order to gain access to the system, then

5 | Let the era of fiat money come to an end

you cannot gain entry. Thus indeed, what you see is that there is hardly anyone in this entire system who is able to receive the higher vision and the love of the Third Ray. For what you will see here is that there is no openness to letting the light flow, to letting money flow.

Money must flow as love

You might wonder, why is it the representatives of the Third Ray of Love who are anchoring their light in the money system? Well, it is indeed because the money system represents love; or rather it *should* represent love. What is love? It is the drive to always transcend, to never stand still—this is what money should be. Money should be always flowing, always multiplying, always adding real value. Then, there should be a constantly growing money supply, but it should be tied to the addition of something that has real value, that raises up life.

What has happened in this nation, and in most other nations, is indeed that life, that the money system, that the flow of the money system has been perverted by the power elites into being a system that stands still, that sits still where there are those who are attempting to control the money supply and the flow of money. You will see that there are many in these United States who advocate a free market economy. There are even those who will claim that the United States *has* a free market economy. There are even those in the Federal Reserve System who will advocate this, even though they surely know better.

There is no other institution in the world who is more dedicated to controlling the free market economy than the Federal Reserve System—because they control the very lifeblood of the economy, namely money itself. What you see is quite simple. The stark reality is that those who scream the loudest about a free market economy are those who are the least dedicated to making it a manifest reality. Indeed, they are the ones who will say that a free market economy will lead to chaos, and thus the government must step in and prevent the collapse of financial institutions that have been built on the clay feet of greed, uncontrolled, unrestricted greed. The reality is that the money system is the problem, not the solution.

Do you need a money system?

Why do you need a money system? Just let the money be regulated by the people themselves. Sure, this will lead to some turmoil, but is that not the only way that people will ever learn? How will they learn if there is a government that seeks to protect them from the consequences of their own choices? In so doing, it becomes an instrument for the elite who are really trying to protect themselves from the consequences of *their* own choices by getting the people to bear the karma for the choices of the elite.

This is one of the fundamental problems of democracy, of any democratic nation. But in few nations is it more important than in these United States, for how can the government be *of* the people, *by* the people and *for* the people unless the people do two things: Number one: educate themselves to the existence of the elite and take a stand for freedom and against elitism. Number two: become willing to bear the consequences of their own choices, instead of expecting the elite to make decisions for them, and their own government to protect them against the consequences of their choices.

What is the purpose of these United States? Is it to provide some physical structure of a great civilization? Is it to provide some degree of welfare or wealth? Or is it to be a path of initiation for as many people as possible? How, then, will anyone learn in the current system where the elite have encaged themselves in these mighty fortresses where they are so insulated from the consequences of their choices, and where they can use the intellectual reasoning to always explain away or outright deny those consequences?

How will the elite learn from this when the people protect them by bearing the consequences of the choices of the elite? How will the elite learn? How will the people learn when the elite has set up a system that also seeks to protect a large part of the people from the consequences of their choices? Do you not see that this is why the elite has allowed the growth of the middle class so that they can get more and more people to feel that they are invested in the stock market or the financial system? So that they will go along with the government when it says that these financial institutions are "too big to fail."

Do you not see what Lanto said about the elite being like the gentleman farmer Thomas Jefferson, who sat at his comfortable estate and was not willing to give up his own slaves, for he did not want to lose his comfortable lifestyle? The elite is like that, but can you not also see that a large part of America's middle class are like that as well? They have now invested for so long that they think they have all this wealth on paper or in numbers on a computer screen. They do not want to lose this good comfortable life, and they are willing to let a large number of their fellow citizens go into the uncertain future of unemployment, just so that they can continue to sit there and enjoy the benefits of the system that is now protected by the government at the cost of increasing unemployment and increasing inflation. Those who have less will have even less, whereas those in the middle class also have less but it really does not matter for they can still be comfortable.

Do you see that as long as there is not that solidarity from the middle class to those who are not as fortunate, well, then the United States cannot be "one nation under God?" For what is needed is that those in the middle class, who have the comfortable lifestyle, dedicate themselves to the spiritual path so that they grasp the higher vision of equality, equal opportunity among all people. They are dedicated to this, and they are willing to sacrifice some of their comfortable lifestyle in order to, so to speak, spread the wealth and give all a more equal opportunity.

Everything that is wrong with the money system

This building, the Federal Reserve Building, represents everything that is wrong, everything that must be transcended, in the money system and the financial system of the United States. Even going beyond to the world where central banks have, again, in almost every nation been a tool for the elite.

We are not here advocating a communist or socialist revolution where the workers stand up against the capitalists. We are advocating a peaceful revolution in higher consciousness where the middle class become the instruments for bringing forth positive change, rather that becoming the buffer zone between the lower classes and the elite.

Can you not see that this is precisely the plan of the elite? They know that, historically speaking, the threat to their rule has always been the lower classes who have little to lose. They have attempted to create a buffer zone between themselves and the lower classes. It is the middle class who now feel that they have a lot to lose. Thus, they are willing to compromise a lot in order to keep their comfortable lifestyle. This is indeed the dilemma, not only of the united States but most industrialized nations. The middle class should be a tool for the growth in consciousness but has now become a hindrance. Because they are so dedicated to worshiping comfortability that they are not willing to become instruments for change.

This cannot continue! If the middle class will not wake up and realize that they have become pawns in a game they do not understand – and then educate themselves to understand this game – well, then the second law of thermodynamics will cause the system to collapse. Until the middle class become the open doors who say: "Show us a higher way; we are willing to see it." Then, again, as Lanto said, when the willingness is there, the help from Above, the ideas from Above, will be readily forthcoming and a new approach to the economy will be released. It has already been released to some degree, but there is not much willingness to listen to those who cry out that fundamental systemic changes are needed in the American economy and financial system. Where is the willingness to listen, I say?

The intensity of the Ruby Fire

Let those who have so far not been willing to listen, let them be awakened by the intensity of this Ruby Fire that is so intense that it is difficult to ignore it. Thus, I speak directly into this building where you sit there, hidden behind your security guards. You think they can protect you against the people, but your henchmen are also *of* the people. There will come a time where you will no longer be able to trust them, as you have already seen in the leaking of documents by those who have access – and must continue to be given access – if you are to be able to continue to run your system.

For systems do not run themselves, they must be run by people. This is the eternal dilemma of the fallen beings and the power elite. They know they cannot trust people so they attempt to build machines and computers that are mechanical and that will carry out their bidding without any conscience. Or they attempt to reduce people to being functionally robots, the mechanized man who has no conscience, who has no heart, and therefore would carry out orders blindly without any humanitarian considerations, or any spiritual considerations.

The myth of equality

This is the consciousness that the Ruby Fire we are anchoring will challenge; not only in this year but beyond this year. We will challenge the consciousness that will not acknowledge that all men are created equal; yet also the consciousness that will not go beyond and recognize that all men are not created equal in the sense that they are the same. They are created equal in the sense that they have equal rights to exist on planet earth, to be in embodiment on planet earth. They have equal rights to pursue Christhood while in embodiment.

What, then, is Christhood? It is the expression of your Divine individuality, for you have become an open door for the flow of love from your Presence. What truly should have been written in the Declaration of Independence – but which Thomas Jefferson was not able to receive because his consciousness was not high enough – is that all men [and women] are created as individuals. They have equal rights to express their individuality, without restricting the expression of the individuality of other people. This is the true principle. Equality is not the principal thing; it is the omega, but the alpha is individuality and the expression of it. Thus, the alpha and the omega of true liberty is individuality and equal rights to express it. This is precisely what must also be incorporated in a functional economy, a golden-age economy. Can you not see that what the elite is trying to do is to prevent individuals from coming up with inventions and ideas that will overthrow the monopoly positions of the elite where they feel they have the economy under control? What they truly fear is the creativity that is the expression of individuality, for they never know when an individual will bring forth and idea or invention that will overthrow their control, or even bring forth an entirely new philosophy, like Jesus did, a philosophy that it took them centuries to bring under their control.

I, Paul the Venetian, and the Archangels and Chohans of the Third Ray, with Sanat Kumara and Venus, I therefore say directly into this Federal Reserve Building and the Federal Reserve System: ENOUGH IS ENOUGH!

Let there be LIGHT, LIGHT, LIGHT, LIGHT, LIGHT, LIGHT, LIGHT! And there IS LIGHT!

Thus, I seal this release and I extend the anchoring of this flame to all other monetary and financial institutions in this Washington, D.C. area. All who in some way come in contact with this nation's money and financial system, will be touched by this Ruby Fire, and by its intensity will be forced to awaken and make the choice between life and death. Will you choose freedom, the free-flow of love and the free-flow of the economy? Or will you choose death—the attempt to control that which cannot be controlled?

Let the people decide what they accept as money. Let the era of fiat money, money by decree, come to an end so that the government cannot be influenced by the elite to force the people to accept money that they have no faith in because it is not tied to anything of real value. Thus, let this system crumble, if the people and the elite are not willing to voluntarily transcend it. We of the Ruby Ray have spoken. It is anchored in the physical octave, and thus, this release is finished.

6 | INVOKING AN END TO THE ERA OF FIAT MONEY

In the name of the I AM THAT I AM, Jesus Christ, I use the authority that I have as a being in embodiment on earth to call upon Paul the Venetian, Elohim Heros, Archangel Chamuel, Sanat Kumara and Venus to reinforce my calls and use my chakras to project the statements in this invocation into the collective consciousness and bring forth the money system of the Golden Age. Awaken Americans to the reality that we are spiritual beings and that we can co-create a new future by working with the ascended masters. I especially call for …

[Make your own calls here.]

Part 1

1. I invoke and multiply the Ruby Fire that is anchored in the Federal Reserve Building and in other centers

around Washington, D.C. that deal with the economy and the finances. I call for this Ruby Fire to serve as the dividing line, as the light of such intensity that it forces people to make the choice between life and death.

> O Heros-Amora, in your love so pink,
> we care not what others about us may think,
> in oneness with you, we claim a new day,
> as innocent children, we frolic and play.

> **O Heros-Amora, we reap what we sow,**
> **yet this is Plan B for helping us grow,**
> **for truly, Plan A is that we join the flow,**
> **immersed in the Infinite Love you bestow.**

2. I call to the loving people of America: "Choose Life!" Choose the life that will get the economy flowing into the golden age matrix, that Saint Germain has prepared for this nation and the world."

> O Heros-Amora, a new life begun,
> we laugh at the devil, the serious one,
> the serpent is stuck in his duality,
> but we are set free by Love's reality.

> **O Heros-Amora, we reap what we sow,**
> **yet this is Plan B for helping us grow,**
> **for truly, Plan A is that we join the flow,**
> **immersed in the Infinite Love you bestow.**

3. I invoke the awakening of the loving people of America to the realization that before this can happen, these monolithic institutions, that attempt to control the money system, must

either transform themselves into non-elitist institutions, or they must be allowed to fail.

> O Heros-Amora, awakened we see,
> in true love is no conditionality,
> we bathe in your glorious Ruby-Pink Sun,
> knowing our God allows life to be fun.

> **O Heros-Amora, we reap what we sow,**
> **yet this is Plan B for helping us grow,**
> **for truly, Plan A is that we join the flow,**
> **immersed in the Infinite Love you bestow.**

4. I invoke the awakening of the loving people of America to the realization that the Federal Reserve Building is "hidden in plain sight," on the National Mall that houses the monuments and institutions of American democracy.

> O Heros-Amora, life is such a joy,
> we see that the world is like a great toy,
> whatever the mind into it projects,
> the mirror of life exactly reflects.

> **O Heros-Amora, we reap what we sow,**
> **yet this is Plan B for helping us grow,**
> **for truly, Plan A is that we join the flow,**
> **immersed in the Infinite Love you bestow.**

5. I invoke the awakening of the loving people of America to the realization that although the Federal Reserve Building has an architecture very similar to that of many government buildings, it is not part of the government that was charged by the

ascended masters with being a government *of* the people, *by* the people and *for* the people.

> O Heros-Amora, conditions you burn,
> we know we are free to take a new turn,
> Immersed in the stream of infinite Love,
> we know that the Spirit came from Above.
>
> **O Heros-Amora, we reap what we sow,**
> **yet this is Plan B for helping us grow,**
> **for truly, Plan A is that we join the flow,**
> **immersed in the Infinite Love you bestow.**

6. I invoke the awakening of the loving people of America to the realization that within the walls of this building, there is very little willingness to be *of* the people, *by* the people and *for* the people.

> O Heros-Amora, we feel that at last,
> we've risen above the trap of the past,
> in true love we claim our freedom to grow,
> forever we're one with Love's Infinite Flow.
>
> **O Heros-Amora, we reap what we sow,**
> **yet this is Plan B for helping us grow,**
> **for truly, Plan A is that we join the flow,**
> **immersed in the Infinite Love you bestow.**

7. I invoke the awakening of the loving people of America to the realization that one gains access to this building only by becoming one of the insiders in the Federal Reserve System.

6 | Invoking an end to the era of fiat money

O Heros-Amora, conditions are ties,
forming a net of serpentine lies,
but you have the antidote setting us free,
you take us beyond conditionality.

**O Heros-Amora, we reap what we sow,
yet this is Plan B for helping us grow,
for truly, Plan A is that we join the flow,
immersed in the Infinite Love you bestow.**

8. I invoke the awakening of the loving people of America to the realization that in order to become an insider, one must have demonstrated a willingness to submit one's individuality to the system. One cannot be a strong individual and enter the banking system that is tied to the Federal Reserve System.

O Heros-Amora, your love is no bond,
for love only wants to take us beyond,
your love has no bounds, forever it flies,
raising all life into Ruby-Pink skies.

**O Heros-Amora, we reap what we sow,
yet this is Plan B for helping us grow,
for truly, Plan A is that we join the flow,
immersed in the Infinite Love you bestow.**

9. I invoke the awakening of the loving people of America to the realization that if one is not willing to submit to the system, to surrender one's individuality in order to gain access to the system, then one cannot gain entry.

O Heros-Amora, love bathing the earth,
filling all people with infinite mirth,
for fear and despair there is no more room,
as all are awakened by love's sonic boom.

**O Heros-Amora, we reap what we sow,
yet this is Plan B for helping us grow,
for truly, Plan A is that we join the flow,
immersed in the Infinite Love you bestow.**

Part 2

1. I invoke the awakening of the loving people of America to the realization that hardly anyone in this entire system is able to receive the higher vision and the love of the Third Ray. There is no openness to letting the light flow, to letting money flow.

O Heros-Amora, in your love so pink,
we care not what others about us may think,
in oneness with you, we claim a new day,
as innocent children, we frolic and play.

**O Heros-Amora, we reap what we sow,
yet this is Plan B for helping us grow,
for truly, Plan A is that we join the flow,
immersed in the Infinite Love you bestow.**

2. I invoke the awakening of the loving people of America to the realization that the money system represents love; or rather it *should* represent love. Love is the drive to always transcend, to never stand still—this is what money should be.

6 | Invoking an end to the era of fiat money

O Heros-Amora, a new life begun,
we laugh at the devil, the serious one,
the serpent is stuck in his duality,
but we are set free by Love's reality.

**O Heros-Amora, we reap what we sow,
yet this is Plan B for helping us grow,
for truly, Plan A is that we join the flow,
immersed in the Infinite Love you bestow.**

3. I invoke the awakening of the loving people of America to the realization that money should be always flowing, always multiplying, always adding real value. There should be a constantly growing money supply, but it should be tied to the addition of something that has real value and raises up life.

O Heros-Amora, awakened we see,
in true love is no conditionality,
we bathe in your glorious Ruby-Pink Sun,
knowing our God allows life to be fun.

**O Heros-Amora, we reap what we sow,
yet this is Plan B for helping us grow,
for truly, Plan A is that we join the flow,
immersed in the Infinite Love you bestow.**

4. I invoke the awakening of the loving people of America to the realization that the money system and the flow of the money system has been perverted by the power elites into being a system that stands still, that sits still where there are those who are attempting to control the money supply and the flow of money.

O Heros-Amora, life is such a joy,
we see that the world is like a great toy,
whatever the mind into it projects,
the mirror of life exactly reflects.

**O Heros-Amora, we reap what we sow,
yet this is Plan B for helping us grow,
for truly, Plan A is that we join the flow,
immersed in the Infinite Love you bestow.**

5. I invoke the awakening of the loving people of America to the realization that many Americans advocate a free market economy and claim that the United States has a free market economy.

O Heros-Amora, conditions you burn,
we know we are free to take a new turn,
Immersed in the stream of infinite Love,
we know that the Spirit came from Above.

**O Heros-Amora, we reap what we sow,
yet this is Plan B for helping us grow,
for truly, Plan A is that we join the flow,
immersed in the Infinite Love you bestow.**

6. I invoke the awakening of the loving people of America to the realization that there is no other institution in the world who is more dedicated to controlling the free market economy than the Federal Reserve System. It controls the very lifeblood of the economy, namely money itself.

O Heros-Amora, we feel that at last,
we've risen above the trap of the past,
in true love we claim our freedom to grow,
forever we're one with Love's Infinite Flow.

O Heros-Amora, we reap what we sow,
yet this is Plan B for helping us grow,
for truly, Plan A is that we join the flow,
immersed in the Infinite Love you bestow.

7. I invoke the awakening of the loving people of America to the realization that those who scream the loudest about a free market economy are those who are the least dedicated to making it a manifest reality.

O Heros-Amora, conditions are ties,
forming a net of serpentine lies,
but you have the antidote setting us free,
you take us beyond conditionality.

O Heros-Amora, we reap what we sow,
yet this is Plan B for helping us grow,
for truly, Plan A is that we join the flow,
immersed in the Infinite Love you bestow.

8. I invoke the awakening of the loving people of America to the realization that some people will say that a free market economy will lead to chaos, and thus the government must step in and prevent the collapse of financial institutions that have been built on the clay feet of uncontrolled, unrestricted greed.

O Heros-Amora, your love is no bond,
for love only wants to take us beyond,
your love has no bounds, forever it flies,
raising all life into Ruby-Pink skies.

**O Heros-Amora, we reap what we sow,
yet this is Plan B for helping us grow,
for truly, Plan A is that we join the flow,
immersed in the Infinite Love you bestow.**

9. I invoke the awakening of the loving people of America to the realization that the money system is the problem, not the solution. We do not necessarily need a money system. We can let the money be regulated by the people themselves. This will lead to some turmoil, but is that not the only way that people will learn?

O Heros-Amora, love bathing the earth,
filling all people with infinite mirth,
for fear and despair there is no more room,
as all are awakened by love's sonic boom.

**O Heros-Amora, we reap what we sow,
yet this is Plan B for helping us grow,
for truly, Plan A is that we join the flow,
immersed in the Infinite Love you bestow.**

Part 3

1. I invoke the awakening of the loving people of America to the realization that people will not learn if there is a government

that seeks to protect them from the consequences of their own choices.

> Chamuel Archangel, in ruby ray power,
> we know we are taking a life-giving shower.
> Love burning away all perversions of will,
> we suddenly feel our desires falling still.
>
> **Chamuel Archangel, descend from Above,**
> **Chamuel Archangel, with ruby-pink love,**
> **Chamuel Archangel, so often thought-of,**
> **Chamuel Archangel, o come Holy Dove.**

2. I invoke the awakening of the loving people of America to the realization that in so doing, the government becomes an instrument for the elite, who are really trying to protect themselves from the consequences of *their* own choices by getting the people to bear the karma for the choices of the elite.

> Chamuel Archangel, a spiral of light,
> as ruby ray fire now pierces the night.
> All forces of darkness consumed by your fire,
> consuming all those who will not rise higher.
>
> **Chamuel Archangel, descend from Above,**
> **Chamuel Archangel, with ruby-pink love,**
> **Chamuel Archangel, so often thought-of,**
> **Chamuel Archangel, o come Holy Dove.**

3. I invoke the awakening of the loving people of America to the realization that elitism is one of the fundamental problems of democracy, and in few nations is it more important than in the United States.

Chamuel Archangel, your love so immense,
with clarified vision, our lives now make sense.
The purpose of life you so clearly reveal,
immersed in your love, God's oneness we feel.

Chamuel Archangel, descend from Above,
Chamuel Archangel, with ruby-pink love,
Chamuel Archangel, so often thought-of,
Chamuel Archangel, o come Holy Dove.

4. I invoke the awakening of the loving people of America to the realization that the government cannot be *of* the people, *by* the people and *for* the people unless the people educate themselves to the existence of the elite and take a stand *for* freedom and *against* elitism.

Chamuel Archangel, what calmness you bring,
we see now that even death has no sting.
For truly, in love there can be no decay,
as love is transcendence into a new day.

Chamuel Archangel, descend from Above,
Chamuel Archangel, with ruby-pink love,
Chamuel Archangel, so often thought-of,
Chamuel Archangel, o come Holy Dove.

5. I invoke the awakening of the loving people of America to the realization that the people must become willing to bear the consequences of their own choices, instead of expecting the elite to make decisions for them, and their own government to protect them against the consequences of their choices.

6 | Invoking an end to the era of fiat money

> Chamuel Archangel, God's Love Flame bestow,
> on all those longing God's true love to know,
> conditions we know can never be real,
> and this is the love you always reveal.

> **Chamuel Archangel, descend from Above,**
> **Chamuel Archangel, with ruby-pink love,**
> **Chamuel Archangel, so often thought-of,**
> **Chamuel Archangel, o come Holy Dove.**

6. I invoke the awakening of the loving people of America to the realization that it is not the purpose of the United States to provide some physical structure of a great civilization. The purpose of the nation is to be a path of initiation for as many people as possible.

> Chamuel Archangel, love's seed you have sown,
> in hearts of all those who don't seek to own,
> for love that possesses is nothing but fear,
> that pierces the heart with duality's spear.

> **Chamuel Archangel, descend from Above,**
> **Chamuel Archangel, with ruby-pink love,**
> **Chamuel Archangel, so often thought-of,**
> **Chamuel Archangel, o come Holy Dove.**

7. I invoke the awakening of the loving people of America to the realization that no one will learn in the current system where the elite have encaged themselves in these mighty fortresses, where they are so insulated from the consequences of their choices, and where they can use the intellectual reasoning to always explain away or outright deny those consequences.

Chamuel Archangel, we don't want control,
for this is the devil's hold on the soul,
your love will now break the serpentine chain,
so we are set free God's love to reclaim.

**Chamuel Archangel, descend from Above,
Chamuel Archangel, with ruby-pink love,
Chamuel Archangel, so often thought-of,
Chamuel Archangel, o come Holy Dove.**

8. I invoke the awakening of the loving people of America to the realization that the elite will not learn when the people protect them by bearing the consequences of the choices of the elite.

Chamuel Archangel, you are so adept,
at helping us God's true love to accept,
we know that the love for which we so yearn,
is not something we on earth have to earn.

**Chamuel Archangel, descend from Above,
Chamuel Archangel, with ruby-pink love,
Chamuel Archangel, so often thought-of,
Chamuel Archangel, o come Holy Dove.**

9. I invoke the awakening of the loving people of America to the realization that the people will not learn when the elite has set up a system that also seeks to protect a large part of the people from the consequences of their choices.

Chamuel Archangel, for love to accept,
we do not need to be so perfect,
for love is not static but always a flow,
demanding only we're willing to grow.

**Chamuel Archangel, descend from Above,
Chamuel Archangel, with ruby-pink love,
Chamuel Archangel, so often thought-of,
Chamuel Archangel, o come Holy Dove.**

Part 4

1. I invoke the awakening of the loving people of America to the realization that the elite has allowed the growth of the middle class so that they can get more and more people to feel that they are invested in the stock market or the financial system. The people will go along with the government when it says that these financial institutions are "too big to fail."

Chamuel Archangel, in ruby ray power,
we know we are taking a life-giving shower.
Love burning away all perversions of will,
we suddenly feel our desires falling still.

**Chamuel Archangel, descend from Above,
Chamuel Archangel, with ruby-pink love,
Chamuel Archangel, so often thought-of,
Chamuel Archangel, o come Holy Dove.**

2. I invoke the awakening of the loving people of America to the realization that the elite do not want to lose this comfortable

lifestyle, but a large part of America's middle class also do not want to lose comfortability.

> Chamuel Archangel, a spiral of light,
> as ruby ray fire now pierces the night.
> All forces of darkness consumed by your fire,
> consuming all those who will not rise higher.

> **Chamuel Archangel, descend from Above,**
> **Chamuel Archangel, with ruby-pink love,**
> **Chamuel Archangel, so often thought-of,**
> **Chamuel Archangel, o come Holy Dove.**

3. I invoke the awakening of the loving people of America to the realization that middle class Americans have now invested for so long that they think they have all this wealth on paper or in numbers on a computer screen. They do not want to lose this good comfortable life.

> Chamuel Archangel, your love so immense,
> with clarified vision, our lives now make sense.
> The purpose of life you so clearly reveal,
> immersed in your love, God's oneness we feel.

> **Chamuel Archangel, descend from Above,**
> **Chamuel Archangel, with ruby-pink love,**
> **Chamuel Archangel, so often thought-of,**
> **Chamuel Archangel, o come Holy Dove.**

4. I invoke the awakening of the loving people of America to the realization that many Americans are willing to let a large number of their fellow citizens go into the uncertain future

of unemployment, just so that they can continue to enjoy the benefits of the system.

> Chamuel Archangel, what calmness you bring,
> we see now that even death has no sting.
> For truly, in love there can be no decay,
> as love is transcendence into a new day.

> **Chamuel Archangel, descend from Above,**
> **Chamuel Archangel, with ruby-pink love,**
> **Chamuel Archangel, so often thought-of,**
> **Chamuel Archangel, o come Holy Dove.**

5. I invoke the awakening of the loving people of America to the realization that the system is now protected by the government at the cost of increasing unemployment and increasing inflation. Those who have less, will have even less, whereas those in the middle class also have less, but they can still be comfortable.

> Chamuel Archangel, God's Love Flame bestow,
> on all those longing God's true love to know,
> conditions we know can never be real,
> and this is the love you always reveal.

> **Chamuel Archangel, descend from Above,**
> **Chamuel Archangel, with ruby-pink love,**
> **Chamuel Archangel, so often thought-of,**
> **Chamuel Archangel, o come Holy Dove.**

6. I invoke the awakening of the loving people of America to the realization that as long as there is not that solidarity from

the middle class to those who are not as fortunate, then the United States cannot be "One Nation under God."

> Chamuel Archangel, love's seed you have sown,
> in hearts of all those who don't seek to own,
> for love that possesses is nothing but fear,
> that pierces the heart with duality's spear.

> **Chamuel Archangel, descend from Above,**
> **Chamuel Archangel, with ruby-pink love,**
> **Chamuel Archangel, so often thought-of,**
> **Chamuel Archangel, o come Holy Dove.**

7. I invoke the awakening of the loving people of America to the realization that what is needed is that those in the middle class, who have the comfortable lifestyle, dedicate themselves to the spiritual path so that they grasp the higher vision of equality, equal opportunity among all people.

> Chamuel Archangel, we don't want control,
> for this is the devil's hold on the soul,
> your love will now break the serpentine chain,
> so we are set free God's love to reclaim.

> **Chamuel Archangel, descend from Above,**
> **Chamuel Archangel, with ruby-pink love,**
> **Chamuel Archangel, so often thought-of,**
> **Chamuel Archangel, o come Holy Dove.**

8. I invoke the awakening of the loving people of America to the realization that only when people are dedicated to this, will they be willing to sacrifice some of their comfortable

lifestyle in order to spread the wealth and give all a more equal opportunity.

> Chamuel Archangel, you are so adept,
> at helping us God's true love to accept,
> we know that the love for which we so yearn,
> is not something we on earth have to earn.

> **Chamuel Archangel, descend from Above,**
> **Chamuel Archangel, with ruby-pink love,**
> **Chamuel Archangel, so often thought-of,**
> **Chamuel Archangel, o come Holy Dove.**

9. I invoke the awakening of the loving people of America to the realization that the Federal Reserve Building represents everything that is wrong, everything that must be transcended, in the money system and the financial system of the United States, even the world where central banks have become a tool for the elite.

> Chamuel Archangel, for love to accept,
> we do not need to be so perfect,
> for love is not static but always a flow,
> demanding only we're willing to grow.

> **Chamuel Archangel, descend from Above,**
> **Chamuel Archangel, with ruby-pink love,**
> **Chamuel Archangel, so often thought-of,**
> **Chamuel Archangel, o come Holy Dove.**

Part 5

1. I invoke the awakening of the loving people of America to the realization that we do not need a communist or socialist revolution where the workers stand up against the capitalists. We call forth a peaceful revolution in higher consciousness where the middle class become the instruments for bringing forth positive change, rather that becoming the buffer zone between the lower classes and the elite.

> Master Paul, venetian dream,
> your love for beauty's flowing stream.
> Master Paul, in love's own womb,
> your power shatters ego's tomb.
>
> **Master Paul, your love so true,**
> **and therefore we apply to you,**
> **to set all free in the great love,**
> **that you are shining from Above.**

2. I invoke the awakening of the loving people of America to the realization that the elite know that, historically speaking, the threat to their rule has always been the lower classes who have little to lose. They have attempted to create a buffer zone between themselves and the lower classes.

> Master Paul, your counsel wise,
> our minds are raised to lofty skies.
> Master Paul, in wisdom's love,
> such beauty flowing from Above.

**Master Paul, your love so true,
and therefore we apply to you,
to set all free in the great love,
that you are shining from Above.**

3. I invoke the awakening of the loving people of America to the realization that the middle class feel that they have a lot to lose, and thus, they are willing to compromise a lot in order to keep their comfortable lifestyle.

Master Paul, love is an art,
it opens up the secret heart.
Master Paul, love's rushing flow,
our hearts awash in sacred glow.

**Master Paul, your love so true,
and therefore we apply to you,
to set all free in the great love,
that you are shining from Above.**

4. I invoke the awakening of the loving people of America to the realization that the dilemma in the United States is that the middle class should be a tool for the growth in consciousness, but it has become a hindrance.

Master Paul, accelerate,
upon pure love we meditate.
Master Paul, intentions pure,
our self-transcendence will ensure.

> **Master Paul, your love so true,**
> **and therefore we apply to you,**
> **to set all free in the great love,**
> **that you are shining from Above.**

5. I invoke the awakening of the loving people of America to the realization that people in the middle class are so dedicated to worshiping comfortability that they are not willing to become instruments for change. This cannot continue!

> Master Paul, your love will heal,
> our inner light you do reveal.
> Master Paul, all life console,
> with you we're being truly whole.

> **Master Paul, your love so true,**
> **and therefore we apply to you,**
> **to set all free in the great love,**
> **that you are shining from Above.**

6. I invoke the awakening of the loving people of America to the realization that if the middle class will not wake up and realize that they have become pawns in a game they do not understand – and then educate themselves to understand this game – then the second law of thermodynamics will cause the system to collapse.

> Master Paul, you serve the All,
> by helping us transcend the fall.
> Master Paul, in peace we rise,
> as ego meets its sure demise.

**Master Paul, your love so true,
and therefore we apply to you,
to set all free in the great love,
that you are shining from Above.**

7. I invoke the awakening of the loving people of America to the realization that the middle class need to become the open doors who say: "Show us a higher way; we are willing to see it."

Master Paul, love all life free,
your love is for eternity.
Master Paul, you are the One,
to help us make the journey fun.

**Master Paul, your love so true,
and therefore we apply to you,
to set all free in the great love,
that you are shining from Above.**

8. I invoke the awakening of the loving people of America to the realization that when the willingness is there, a new approach to the economy will be released. But there must be a willingness to listen to those who cry out that fundamental systemic changes are needed in the American economy and financial system.

Master Paul, you balance all,
the seven rays upon our call.
Master Paul, you paint the sky,
with colors that delight the I.

> **Master Paul, your love so true,**
> **and therefore we apply to you,**
> **to set all free in the great love,**
> **that you are shining from Above.**

9. I call for those who have so far not been willing to listen, to be awakened by the intensity of the Ruby Fire that is so intense that it is difficult to ignore it.

> Master Paul, your Presence here,
> filling up the inner sphere.
> Life is now a sacred flow,
> God Love we do on all bestow.

> **Master Paul, your love so true,**
> **and therefore we apply to you,**
> **to set all free in the great love,**
> **that you are shining from Above.**

Part 6

1. I speak directly into this building, where you sit there, hidden behind your security guards. You think they can protect you against the people, but your henchmen are also of the people.

> Sanat Kumara, Ruby Fire,
> I seek my place in love's own choir,
> with open hearts we sing your praise,
> together we the earth do raise.

6 | Invoking an end to the era of fiat money

**Sanat Kumara, Ruby Ray,
bring to earth a higher way,
light this planet with your fire,
clothe her in a new attire.**

2. I call forth a time where the elite will no longer be able to trust their employees, as in the leaking of documents by those who have access – and must continue to be given access – if the elite is to be able to continue to run their system.

Sanat Kumara, Ruby Fire,
initiations I desire,
I am for you an electrode,
Shamballa is my true abode.

**Sanat Kumara, Ruby Ray,
bring to earth a higher way,
light this planet with your fire,
clothe her in a new attire.**

3. I invoke the awakening of the loving people of America to the realization that systems do not run themselves, they must be run by people. This is the eternal dilemma of the fallen beings and the power elite.

Sanat Kumara, Ruby Fire,
I follow path that you require,
initiate me with your love,
the open door for Holy Dove.

> **Sanat Kumara, Ruby Ray,**
> **bring to earth a higher way,**
> **light this planet with your fire,**
> **clothe her in a new attire.**

4. I invoke the awakening of the loving people of America to the realization that the elite know they cannot trust people, so they attempt to build machines and computers that are mechanical and that will carry out their bidding without any conscience.

> Sanat Kumara, Ruby Fire,
> your great example all inspire,
> with non-attachment and great mirth,
> we give the earth a true rebirth.

> **Sanat Kumara, Ruby Ray,**
> **bring to earth a higher way,**
> **light this planet with your fire,**
> **clothe her in a new attire.**

5. I invoke the awakening of the loving people of America to the realization that the elite attempt to reduce people to being functionally robots, the mechanized man who has no conscience, who has no heart, and therefore would carry out orders blindly without any humanitarian considerations, or any spiritual considerations.

> Sanat Kumara, Ruby Fire,
> you are this planet's purifier,
> consume on earth all spirits dark,
> reveal the inner Spirit Spark.

**Sanat Kumara, Ruby Ray,
bring to earth a higher way,
light this planet with your fire,
clothe her in a new attire.**

6. I call for the Ruby Fire anchored here to challenge the elitist consciousness, and the mechanization consciousness that will not acknowledge that all men are created equal.

Sanat Kumara, Ruby Fire,
you are a cosmic amplifier,
the lower forces can't withstand,
vibrations from Venusian band.

**Sanat Kumara, Ruby Ray,
bring to earth a higher way,
light this planet with your fire,
clothe her in a new attire.**

7. I call for the Ruby Fire to challenge the consciousness that will not recognize that all men are not created equal in the sense that they are the same. They are created equal in the sense that they have equal rights to be in embodiment on planet earth. And they have equal rights to pursue Christhood while in embodiment.

Sanat Kumara, Ruby Fire,
I am on earth your magnifier,
the flow of love I do restore,
my chakras are your open door.

**Sanat Kumara, Ruby Ray,
bring to earth a higher way,
light this planet with your fire,
clothe her in a new attire.**

8. I invoke the awakening of the loving people of America to the realization that Christhood is the expression of our Divine individuality, for we have become an open door for the flow of love from the Presence.

Sanat Kumara, Ruby Fire,
Venusian song the multiplier,
as we your love reverberate,
the densest minds we penetrate.

**Sanat Kumara, Ruby Ray,
bring to earth a higher way,
light this planet with your fire,
clothe her in a new attire.**

9. I invoke the awakening of the loving people of America to the realization that what truly should have been written in the Declaration of Independence is that all humans are created as individuals, and they have equal rights to express their individuality, without restricting the expression of the individuality of other people.

Sanat Kumara, Ruby Fire,
you are for all the sanctifier,
the earth is now a holy place,
purified by cosmic grace.

**Sanat Kumara, Ruby Ray,
bring to earth a higher way,
light this planet with your fire,
clothe her in a new attire.**

Part 7

1. I invoke the awakening of the loving people of America to the realization that equality is not the principal thing; it is the omega, but the alpha is individuality and the expression of it.

> O Venus, show me how to serve,
> your cosmic beauty I observe.
> What love from Venus you now bring,
> our planets do in tandem sing.

> **O Venus, service so divine,
> you are for earth a cosmic sign.
> Your selfless service is now mine,
> a life in service I define.**

2. I invoke the awakening of the loving people of America to the realization that the alpha and the omega of true liberty is individuality and equal rights to express it. This is precisely what must also be incorporated in a functional economy, a golden age economy.

> O Venus, your love is the key,
> the hardened hearts on earth are free.
> Embracing future bright and bold,
> our planet's story is retold.

> **O Venus, service so divine,**
> **you are for earth a cosmic sign.**
> **Your selfless service is now mine,**
> **a life in service I define.**

3. I invoke the awakening of the loving people of America to the realization that what the elite is trying to do is to prevent individuals from coming up with inventions and ideas that will overthrow the monopoly positions of the elite who feel they have the economy under control.

> O Venus, loving Mother mine,
> my heart your love does now refine.
> I am the open door for love,
> descending like a Holy Dove.

> **O Venus, service so divine,**
> **you are for earth a cosmic sign.**
> **Your selfless service is now mine,**
> **a life in service I define.**

4. I invoke the awakening of the loving people of America to the realization that what members of the elite fear is the creativity that is the expression of individuality. For they never know when an individual will bring forth and idea or invention that will overthrow their control.

> O Venus, play the secret note,
> that is for hatred antidote.
> All poisoned hearts you gently heal,
> as love's true story you reveal.

**O Venus, service so divine,
you are for earth a cosmic sign.
Your selfless service is now mine,
a life in service I define.**

5. I call for the extension of the Ruby Fire to all other monetary and financial institutions in the Washington, D.C. area, so that all who come in contact with this nation's money and financial system, will be touched by this Ruby Fire.

O Venus, love fills every need,
for truly, love is God's first seed.
O let it blossom, let it grow,
sweep earth into your loving flow.

**O Venus, service so divine,
you are for earth a cosmic sign.
Your selfless service is now mine,
a life in service I define.**

6. I call for all people who come in contact with this Ruby Fire to awaken and make the choice between life and death. Choose freedom, the free flow of love and the free flow of the economy.

O Venus, music of the spheres,
heard by those who God reveres.
Our voices now as one we raise,
singing in adoring praise.

> **O Venus, service so divine,**
> **you are for earth a cosmic sign.**
> **Your selfless service is now mine,**
> **a life in service I define.**

7. I invoke the awakening of the loving people of America to the realization that death is the attempt to control that which cannot be controlled. We need to let the people decide what they accept as money.

> O Venus, we are joining ranks,
> Sanat Kumara we give thanks.
> Our planet has received new life,
> to lift her out of war and strife.

> **O Venus, service so divine,**
> **you are for earth a cosmic sign.**
> **Your selfless service is now mine,**
> **a life in service I define.**

8. I invoke the awakening of the loving people of America to the realization that we need to let the era of fiat money, money by decree, come to an end, so that the government cannot be influenced by the elite to force the people to accept money that they have no faith in because it is not tied to anything of real value.

> O Venus, your sweet melody,
> consumes veil of duality.
> Absorbed in tones of Cosmic Love,
> all conflict we now rise above.

> O Venus, service so divine,
> you are for earth a cosmic sign.
> Your selfless service is now mine,
> a life in service I define.

9. I invoke the awakening of the loving people of America to the realization that we need to let this system crumble, if the people and the elite are not willing to voluntarily transcend it.

> O Venus, shining Morning Star,
> a cosmic herald, that you are.
> The earth set free by sacred sound,
> our planet is now heaven-bound.

> **O Venus, service so divine,
> you are for earth a cosmic sign.
> Your selfless service is now mine,
> a life in service I define.**

By the authority of the Christ within me and in oneness with Paul the Venetian, and the Archangels and Chohans of the Third Ray, with Sanat Kumara and Venus I say directly into this Federal Reserve Building and the Federal Reserve System: ENOUGH IS ENOUGH!

Let there be LIGHT, LIGHT, LIGHT, LIGHT, LIGHT, LIGHT, LIGHT! And there *is* LIGHT!

Sealing

In the name of the I AM THAT I AM, I accept that Archangel Michael, Astrea and Shiva form an impenetrable shield around myself and all constructive people, sealing us from all fear-based energies in all four octaves. I accept that the Light of God is consuming and transforming all fear-based energies that make up the dark forces working against America!

7 | THE TRUE ALCHEMY OF ACCELERATION

This dictation was given at the Washington Monument in Washington, D.C.

Serapis Bey I AM, and I AM here through the physical presence of this messenger to anchor the light of the Fourth Ray, but not the Fourth Ray of purity as many students think. I AM here to anchor the higher aspect of the Fourth Ray of purity, namely that of acceleration.

Light is the alchemical key. Light is the philosopher's stone. Light is the missing ingredient that the alchemists have been seeking, mostly in vain, for centuries. Light is the ingredient that can accelerate what is below, but it must be light that comes from Above. Thus, it is the Christ light that they seek; those who have an honest desire for self-transformation, as opposed to those who have a self-centered, the separate self centered, desire to attain power. They want to take heaven by force and use the light to advance some personal agenda that seems important to the separate self but does nothing to raise the All.

Understanding Christ light

Surely, light is the key. This you can all see, but many of you, who have been students of the ascended masters for a long time, tend to think that there is only one Christ light, that the Christ light might have a certain vibration or certain qualities that can magically transform whatever is below. Yet this is, while not incorrect, not a complete understanding. There is not one form of Christ light; there is not one vibration of Christ light, for what is the purpose of the Christ light? It is to accelerate any condition in the material realm, not to some ultimate level, for that would in many cases burn and destroy what is below. It is to take any form that is below and accelerate it to the next level up so that the people who are at a certain level of consciousness will transcend that level and be accelerated to the next level—if they are willing to take in the Christ light and let it perform the alchemy that it has the potential to perform.

Thus, there are many forms of Christ light. For each manifestation that you have in the lower realm, there is a certain form of Christ light that will help that manifestation transcend the level of consciousness from which it springs; out of which it is a manifestation. We give the teaching that there are 144 distinct levels of consciousness possible in the material frequency spectrum on earth. There are 144 different levels, different vibrations, different aspects of the Christ light.

Thus, you might, if you want to have a visible representation of the Christ light, see it as a pyramid, a pyramid that ends up being multi-faceted, like a diamond that has 144 facets. Yet what is that pyramid – as you see on the top of this Washington Monument here in Washington, D.C. – what is the essential characteristic of a pyramid? Well, it is the alpha and the omega. It has four sides, representing the four levels of the material universe, the circle that has been squared into manifestation.

Yet, at the top of the pyramid, you find what? You find the single point, you find the singularity that represents the fact that you come into a state where your awareness, your sense of self, is not pulled into any of the four levels of matter and has, in fact, transcended identification with any of the 144 levels of consciousness possible in the matter realm.

Thus, you have become the singularity, the open door, the Conscious You experiencing itself as pure awareness instead of experiencing the world of form through one of the 144 levels of consciousness. This is the alchemical symbol, and it is only when you step away from a certain level of the 144 possible – transcend that at least momentarily – and experience the pure awareness of coming into the single-eyed vision (the single-eyed sense of self) that you become the open door for the Christ light to descend in a manifestation that can transform you, that can help you accelerate to the next level of consciousness up. Or can help other people, even an entire society, accelerate to that next level up.

Being an alchemist

This is what it means to be an alchemist. It is not a matter of finding a secret formula; a secret word or some kind of hocus-pocus, or black magic, or white magic, or grey magic, or pink magic or whatever you might imagine for magic.

It is a matter of coming into the singularity. For only when you are in pure awareness, can you see your current level of consciousness from the outside. Only when you realize that you are more than that level of consciousness, can you transcend that level of consciousness.

What does it take for *you* to come into the singularity? You must be willing to accelerate yourself beyond your current level of consciousness, and what does it take to do that? It takes that you make a decision! It is not a matter of giving violet flame for 20 years, and then one day you will magically be transformed into a higher level of consciousness. It is not a matter of chanting this or chanting that, eating this or not eating that; performing some kind of occult or obscure rituals. It is a matter of you coming to a point where you decide that you have had enough of the old state of consciousness and thus you deliberately, willingly, and consciously accelerate your awareness.

Some of you will say: "Well, how do we do this, Serapis Bey? Just tell us how, give us the magical formula!" Have I not just said there is no magical formula? It is a decision. *You* must make the decision. If you do not know how to make a decision, then I suggest you do not consider yourself a student of the Fourth Ray of acceleration. For indeed, all of you, if you are willing to acknowledge it, know how to make decisions, for you make decisions all the time. It is, of course, not a matter of making a decision with the outer mind; it is a matter of knowing how to still the outer mind so that the decision comes from your I Will Be Presence. You tune in to what the Presence desires to express through you that is higher than what you are expressing right now.

Then, you make that decision to embrace the higher, to accept it, to let it transform you, and therefore give up whatever old habits you need to give up in order to flow with the energy impulse, the River of Life, from your I Will Be Presence. This is the key; not some magical formula, not some secret ritual like they seek in whatever secret societies or not secret societies they have. Even the people who built this monument, who thought they encoded great wisdom in it, yet was it wisdom that helped them transcend? Or was it wisdom that helped them justify staying at a certain level of consciousness where they felt wiser than others, where they felt that they were the wise ones because they knew the secret wisdom that the ordinary man did not know and which these people thought the ordinary man could not comprehend.

Is it a matter of comprehending some advanced wisdom? Or is it a matter of the purity of the heart, the acceleration of the heart, the willingness to go beyond that which is, and become more, and manifest the more, flow with the more, be the open door for the more?

This is the key to alchemy; not some secret formula, where you seek to attain some advanced state or wisdom in order to build up the separate self and its ever-moving, never-satisfiable quest for superiority compared to others on a relative, dualistic scale that has no reality in the Christ light. For when the Christ light shines, you see the futility of these dualistic measurements and scales that men have set up in order to feel they are more important than others.

The light that penetrates the thickest walls

This, then, is what I represent as the hierarch of the Fourth Ray, and this is the light that I have anchored here during this dictation. I have anchored a light that will spread from the very top of the pyramid on this monument that will spread out through Washington, D.C. in all directions, that will go through every government building no matter how thick the walls they have built, no matter the fortresses they have attempted to build to prevent themselves from being listened to by electronic equipment of any kind that they think they have invented or that others have invented.

All of this means nothing to the Christ light, for it penetrates it all. Thus, it will go right in and challenge these institutions that have become so entrapped in the dualistic consciousness that they feel threatened by just about anything that they do not understand or feel they cannot control. They are, when you look at some of these buildings in or around this Mall, they are like the medieval fortresses with thick walls – or thick firewalls – that they have built in order to keep others out—supposedly. But really, it is in order to keep themselves in so that they feel they do not have to change because they have to respond to these real or imagined threats.

Thus, they are trapped in the dualistic consciousness, which is where they want to be. For they do not want to change, they do not want to look at themselves, they do not want to transcend. Thus, you cannot be an alchemist. You may think that the medieval alchemists were pursuing the goal of transforming lead into gold so that they could be rich or powerful, you may think they were attempting to gain some outer power. Indeed, some of them were, but that was because they had not understood the purpose of alchemy.

You cannot transform anything outside of yourself, if you are not willing to transform yourself. You do not *find* a secret formula. If you are a true alchemist, you *become* the formula. Because you become the open door for the light, and the light is what does the work, and it cannot be forced by any matrix or structure on earth. Like you will hear the wind blowing, the Holy Spirit bloweth where it listeth, for it will always challenge the structure, whatever structure, and compel it to transcend and compel those who are trapped in the structure to transcend and realize they are more than any structure. For they are God-free spiritual beings with unlimited free will to define any self for themselves that they are capable of and willing to imagine.

If you do not dare to imagine, then you cannot be an alchemist. You cannot transcend that which is already manifest, if you dare not imagine anything beyond it, anything that is more.

7 | *The true alchemy of acceleration*

This is the reality of the Fourth Ray; this is the reality I teach at my Temple at Luxor, at least for those who have passed the kindergarten stage where they are no longer seeking to convert or convince others or to out-compete them by somehow becoming better than others.

Becoming more does not mean becoming more than others or becoming more compared to any relative scale. It means transcending – going beyond – anything that already is. You may think you can define some perfection, and when you have that perfection you no longer need to transcend. Nay, it is not so.

Did not Christ have to die on the cross? Did he not have to give up the ghost before he could die and be reborn? Thus, do you not see there is no ultimate state on earth, from which you do not have to transcend yourself? Give up this dream of the fallen consciousness of some ultimate state where you do not need to transcend and become more. Let it go and then you will know the alchemy of the Fourth Ray. Thus, I have spoken. I have anchored my light and I have given you an essential teaching for those who are willing to understand it, but go beyond understanding it, and letting it infuse their consciousness and accelerate them to the point where they can make that decision to accelerate to a higher level of consciousness. Thus, it is sealed. Serapis I AM!

8 | INVOKING THE ALCHEMY OF ACCELERATION

In the name of the I AM THAT I AM, Jesus Christ, I use the authority that I have as a being in embodiment on earth to call upon Serapis Bey to reinforce my calls and use my chakras to project the statements in this invocation into the collective consciousness and awaken Americans to the need to accelerate our consciousness beyond duality. Awaken Americans to the reality that we are spiritual beings and that we can co-create a new future by working with the ascended masters. I especially call for ...

[Make your own calls here.]

Part 1

1. I invoke the awakening of the progressive people of America to the realization that light is the alchemical key. Light is the philosopher's stone. Light is the

missing ingredient that the alchemists have been seeking for centuries.

> Beloved Astrea, your heart is so true,
> your Circle and Sword of white and blue,
> cut all life free from dramas unwise,
> on wings of Purity our planet will rise.
>
> **Beloved Astrea, in oneness with you,**
> **your circle and sword of electric blue,**
> **with Purity's Light cutting right through,**
> **raising the earth into all that is true.**

2. I invoke the awakening of the progressive people of America to the realization that light is the ingredient that can accelerate what is below, but it must be light that comes from Above.

> Beloved Astrea, in God Purity,
> accelerate all of our life energy,
> we're rising beyond every impurity,
> as Purity's Light forever we see.
>
> **Beloved Astrea, in oneness with you,**
> **your circle and sword of electric blue,**
> **with Purity's Light cutting right through,**
> **raising the earth into all that is true.**

3. I invoke the awakening of the progressive people of America to the realization that it is the Christ light that we seek, those of us who have an honest desire for self-transformation, as opposed to those who have a self-centered desire to attain power.

8 | Invoking the alchemy of acceleration

Beloved Astrea, from Purity's Ray,
send forth deliverance to all life today,
acceleration to Purity, we are now free
from all that is less than love's Purity.

Beloved Astrea, in oneness with you,
your circle and sword of electric blue,
with Purity's Light cutting right through,
raising the earth into all that is true.

4. I invoke the awakening of the progressive people of America to the realization that there is not one form of Christ light; there is not one vibration of Christ light.

Beloved Astrea, accelerate us all,
as for your deliverance we fervently call,
set all life free from vision impure
beyond fear and doubt, we're rising for sure.

Beloved Astrea, in oneness with you,
your circle and sword of electric blue,
with Purity's Light cutting right through,
raising the earth into all that is true.

5. I invoke the awakening of the progressive people of America to the realization that the purpose of the Christ light is to accelerate any condition in the material realm, but not to some ultimate level for that would burn and destroy what is below.

Beloved Astrea, we're willing to see,
all of the lies that keep us unfree,
we surrender all lies causing the fall,
forever affirming the oneness of All.

> **Beloved Astrea, in oneness with you,**
> **your circle and sword of electric blue,**
> **with Purity's Light cutting right through,**
> **raising the earth into all that is true.**

6. I invoke the awakening of the progressive people of America to the realization that the purpose of the light is to take any form that is below and accelerate it to the next level up.

> Beloved Astrea, accelerate life
> beyond all duality's struggle and strife,
> consume all division between God and man,
> accelerate fulfillment of God's perfect plan.

> **Beloved Astrea, in oneness with you,**
> **your circle and sword of electric blue,**
> **with Purity's Light cutting right through,**
> **raising the earth into all that is true.**

7. I invoke the awakening of the progressive people of America to the realization that the purpose of the light is to take people who are at a certain level of consciousness and help them transcend that level and be accelerated to the next level.

> Beloved Astrea, we lovingly call,
> break down separation's invisible wall,
> raising our minds into true unity
> with the Masters of love in Infinity.

> **Beloved Astrea, in oneness with you,**
> **your circle and sword of electric blue,**
> **with Purity's Light cutting right through,**
> **raising the earth into all that is true.**

8 | Invoking the alchemy of acceleration

8. I invoke the awakening of the progressive people of America to the realization that there are many forms of Christ light. For each manifestation that we have in the lower realm, there is a certain form of Christ light that will help that manifestation transcend the level of consciousness from which it springs.

> Beloved Astrea, help all of us find,
> the secret that we create with the mind,
> and thus what in ignorance we decreate,
> in knowledge we easily can recreate.

> **Beloved Astrea, in oneness with you,**
> **your circle and sword of electric blue,**
> **with Purity's Light cutting right through,**
> **raising the earth into all that is true.**

9. I invoke the awakening of the progressive people of America to the realization that there are 144 distinct levels of consciousness possible in the material frequency spectrum on earth. Thus, there are 144 different aspects of the Christ light.

> Beloved Astrea, we all do aspire,
> to learning to use your purity's fire,
> to raise every form in infamy sown,
> as Saint Germain makes this planet his own.

> **Beloved Astrea, in oneness with you,**
> **your circle and sword of electric blue,**
> **with Purity's Light cutting right through,**
> **raising the earth into all that is true.**

Part 2

1. I invoke the awakening of the progressive people of America to the realization that the Christ light is like a pyramid that ends up being multi-faceted, like a diamond that has 144 facets.

> Beloved Astrea, your heart is so true,
> your Circle and Sword of white and blue,
> cut all life free from dramas unwise,
> on wings of Purity our planet will rise.
>
> **Beloved Astrea, in oneness with you,**
> **your circle and sword of electric blue,**
> **with Purity's Light cutting right through,**
> **raising the earth into all that is true.**

2. I invoke the awakening of the progressive people of America to the realization that the essential characteristic of a pyramid is the alpha and the omega. It has four sides, representing the four levels of the material universe, the circle that has been squared into manifestation.

> Beloved Astrea, in God Purity,
> accelerate all of our life energy,
> we're rising beyond every impurity,
> as Purity's Light forever we see.
>
> **Beloved Astrea, in oneness with you,**
> **your circle and sword of electric blue,**
> **with Purity's Light cutting right through,**
> **raising the earth into all that is true.**

8 | Invoking the alchemy of acceleration

3. I invoke the awakening of the progressive people of America to the realization that at the top of the pyramid we find the single point, the singularity.

> Beloved Astrea, from Purity's Ray,
> send forth deliverance to all life today,
> acceleration to Purity, we are now free
> from all that is less than love's Purity.
>
> **Beloved Astrea, in oneness with you,**
> **your circle and sword of electric blue,**
> **with Purity's Light cutting right through,**
> **raising the earth into all that is true.**

4. I invoke the awakening of the progressive people of America to the realization that the singularity represents the fact that we come into a state where our awareness, our sense of self, is not pulled into any of the four levels of matter.

> Beloved Astrea, accelerate us all,
> as for your deliverance we fervently call,
> set all life free from vision impure
> beyond fear and doubt, we're rising for sure.
>
> **Beloved Astrea, in oneness with you,**
> **your circle and sword of electric blue,**
> **with Purity's Light cutting right through,**
> **raising the earth into all that is true.**

5. I invoke the awakening of the progressive people of America to the realization that we can transcend identification with any of the 144 levels of consciousness possible in the matter realm.

> Beloved Astrea, we're willing to see,
> all of the lies that keep us unfree,
> we surrender all lies causing the fall,
> forever affirming the oneness of All.
>
> **Beloved Astrea, in oneness with you,**
> **your circle and sword of electric blue,**
> **with Purity's Light cutting right through,**
> **raising the earth into all that is true.**

6. I invoke the awakening of the progressive people of America to the realization that we then become the singularity, the open door, the Conscious You experiencing itself as pure awareness instead of experiencing the world of form through one of the 144 levels of consciousness.

> Beloved Astrea, accelerate life
> beyond all duality's struggle and strife,
> consume all division between God and man,
> accelerate fulfillment of God's perfect plan.
>
> **Beloved Astrea, in oneness with you,**
> **your circle and sword of electric blue,**
> **with Purity's Light cutting right through,**
> **raising the earth into all that is true.**

7. I invoke the awakening of the progressive people of America to the realization that we become the open door only when we step away from a certain level of the 144 levels and experience the pure awareness of coming into the single-eyed vision, the single-eyed sense of self.

> Beloved Astrea, we lovingly call,
> break down separation's invisible wall,
> raising our minds into true unity
> with the Masters of love in Infinity.
>
> **Beloved Astrea, in oneness with you,**
> **your circle and sword of electric blue,**
> **with Purity's Light cutting right through,**
> **raising the earth into all that is true.**

8. I invoke the awakening of the progressive people of America to the realization that when our vision is single, we become the open door for the Christ light to descend into manifestation.

> Beloved Astrea, help all of us find,
> the secret that we create with the mind,
> and thus what in ignorance we decreate,
> in knowledge we easily can recreate.
>
> **Beloved Astrea, in oneness with you,**
> **your circle and sword of electric blue,**
> **with Purity's Light cutting right through,**
> **raising the earth into all that is true.**

9. I invoke the awakening of the progressive people of America to the realization that the Christ light can transform us, can help us accelerate to the next level of consciousness. It can help other people, even an entire society, accelerate to the next level up.

Beloved Astrea, we all do aspire,
to learning to use your purity's fire,
to raise every form in infamy sown,
as Saint Germain makes this planet his own.

Beloved Astrea, in oneness with you,
your circle and sword of electric blue,
with Purity's Light cutting right through,
raising the earth into all that is true.

Part 3

1. I invoke the awakening of the progressive people of America to the realization that being an alchemist is not a matter of finding a secret formula, a secret word or some kind of magic. Being an alchemist is a matter of coming into the singularity.

Gabriel Archangel, your light we revere,
immersed in your Presence, nothing we fear.
Disciples of Christ, we do leave behind,
the ego's desire for responding in kind.

Gabriel Archangel, of this we are sure,
Gabriel Archangel, Christ light is the cure.
Gabriel Archangel, intentions so pure,
Gabriel Archangel, in you we're secure.

2. I invoke the awakening of the progressive people of America to the realization that only when we are in pure awareness, can we see our current level of consciousness from the outside.

8 | Invoking the alchemy of acceleration

And only when we realize that we are more than that level of consciousness, can we transcend that level of consciousness.

> Gabriel Archangel, we fear not the light,
> in purifications' fire, we delight.
> With your hand in ours, each challenge we face,
> we follow the spiral to infinite grace.

Gabriel Archangel, of this we are sure,
Gabriel Archangel, Christ light is the cure.
Gabriel Archangel, intentions so pure,
Gabriel Archangel, in you we're secure.

3. I invoke the awakening of the progressive people of America to the realization that in order to come into the singularity, we must be willing to accelerate ourselves beyond our current level of consciousness.

> Gabriel Archangel, your fire burning white,
> ascending with you, out of the night.
> The ego has nowhere to run and to hide,
> in ascension's bright spiral, with you we abide.

Gabriel Archangel, of this we are sure,
Gabriel Archangel, Christ light is the cure.
Gabriel Archangel, intentions so pure,
Gabriel Archangel, in you we're secure.

4. I invoke the awakening of the progressive people of America to the realization that in order to do that, we must make a decision! We must decide that we have had enough of the old state of consciousness and thus we deliberately, willingly and consciously accelerate our awareness.

Gabriel Archangel, your trumpet we hear,
announcing the birth of Christ drawing near.
In lightness of being, we now are reborn,
rising with Christ on bright Easter morn.

Gabriel Archangel, of this we are sure,
Gabriel Archangel, Christ light is the cure.
Gabriel Archangel, intentions so pure,
Gabriel Archangel, in you we're secure.

5. I invoke the awakening of the progressive people of America to the realization that it is not a matter of making a decision with the outer mind; it is a matter of knowing how to still the outer mind so that the decision comes from the Presence.

Gabriel Archangel, the earth is now free,
embracing a nondual reality,
the judgment of Christ upon forces so dark,
who deny that all have a spiritual spark.

Gabriel Archangel, of this we are sure,
Gabriel Archangel, Christ light is the cure.
Gabriel Archangel, intentions so pure,
Gabriel Archangel, in you we're secure.

6. I invoke the awakening of the progressive people of America to the realization that we need to tune in to what the Presence desires to express through us, which is higher than what we are expressing right now.

8 | Invoking the alchemy of acceleration

> Gabriel Archangel, with angels so white,
> raising our planet out of the dark night,
> as we now intone the Word of the Lord,
> the beings who fell are bound by your sword.
>
> **Gabriel Archangel, of this we are sure,**
> **Gabriel Archangel, Christ light is the cure.**
> **Gabriel Archangel, intentions so pure,**
> **Gabriel Archangel, in you we're secure.**

7. I invoke the awakening of the progressive people of America to the realization that we then make the decision to embrace the higher, to accept it, to let it transform us, and therefore give up whatever old habits we need to give up in order to flow with the River of Life.

> Gabriel Archangel, we call now to you,
> the astral plane your light burning through,
> entities, demons, discarnates are bound,
> as you and we intone Sacred Sound.
>
> **Gabriel Archangel, of this we are sure,**
> **Gabriel Archangel, Christ light is the cure.**
> **Gabriel Archangel, intentions so pure,**
> **Gabriel Archangel, in you we're secure.**

8. I invoke the awakening of the progressive people of America to the realization that we need to give up the wisdom that helps us justify staying at a certain level of consciousness where we feel wiser than others.

Gabriel Archangel, what glorious day,
your radiant angels have come here to stay,
your purifications fire burning white,
intentions so pure, our hearts taking flight.

Gabriel Archangel, of this we are sure,
Gabriel Archangel, Christ light is the cure.
Gabriel Archangel, intentions so pure,
Gabriel Archangel, in you we're secure.

9. I invoke the awakening of the progressive people of America to the realization that it is not a matter of comprehending some advanced wisdom. It is a matter of the purity of the heart, the acceleration of the heart, the willingness to go beyond that which is, and become more, and manifest the more, flow with the more, be the open door for the more.

Gabriel Archangel, our planet so pure,
in our bright new future we do feel secure,
with your band of light encircling the earth,
Saint Germain's Golden Age is now given birth.

Gabriel Archangel, of this we are sure,
Gabriel Archangel, Christ light is the cure.
Gabriel Archangel, intentions so pure,
Gabriel Archangel, in you we're secure.

Part 4

1. I invoke the awakening of the progressive people of America to the realization that alchemy is not about seeking to attain

some advanced state or wisdom in order to build up the separate self and its ever-moving, never-satisfiable quest for superiority compared to others on a relative, dualistic scale.

> Gabriel Archangel, your light we revere,
> immersed in your Presence, nothing we fear.
> Disciples of Christ, we do leave behind,
> the ego's desire for responding in kind.
>
> **Gabriel Archangel, of this we are sure,**
> **Gabriel Archangel, Christ light is the cure.**
> **Gabriel Archangel, intentions so pure,**
> **Gabriel Archangel, in you we're secure.**

2. I invoke the awakening of the progressive people of America to the realization that when the Christ light shines, we see the futility of these dualistic measurements and scales that men have set up in order to feel they are more important than others.

> Gabriel Archangel, we fear not the light,
> in purifications' fire, we delight.
> With your hand in ours, each challenge we face,
> we follow the spiral to infinite grace.
>
> **Gabriel Archangel, of this we are sure,**
> **Gabriel Archangel, Christ light is the cure.**
> **Gabriel Archangel, intentions so pure,**
> **Gabriel Archangel, in you we're secure.**

3. I call forth the light that Serapis Bey has anchored over the Washington Monument, and I call for it to spread out through Washington, D.C. in all directions.

Gabriel Archangel, your fire burning white,
ascending with you, out of the night.
The ego has nowhere to run and to hide,
in ascension's bright spiral, with you we abide.

Gabriel Archangel, of this we are sure,
Gabriel Archangel, Christ light is the cure.
Gabriel Archangel, intentions so pure,
Gabriel Archangel, in you we're secure.

4. I call for the light of Serapis Bey to go through every government building no matter how thick the walls they have built, no matter the fortresses they have attempted to build to prevent themselves from being listened to by electronic equipment of any kind.

Gabriel Archangel, your trumpet we hear,
announcing the birth of Christ drawing near.
In lightness of being, we now are reborn,
rising with Christ on bright Easter morn.

Gabriel Archangel, of this we are sure,
Gabriel Archangel, Christ light is the cure.
Gabriel Archangel, intentions so pure,
Gabriel Archangel, in you we're secure.

5. I call for the Christ light to penetrate all and to challenge these institutions that have become so entrapped in the dualistic consciousness that they feel threatened by anything that they do not understand or feel they cannot control.

8 | Invoking the alchemy of acceleration

> Gabriel Archangel, the earth is now free,
> embracing a nondual reality,
> the judgment of Christ upon forces so dark,
> who deny that all have a spiritual spark.
>
> **Gabriel Archangel, of this we are sure,**
> **Gabriel Archangel, Christ light is the cure.**
> **Gabriel Archangel, intentions so pure,**
> **Gabriel Archangel, in you we're secure.**

6. I call for the Christ light to challenge those who have built thick walls, supposedly in order to keep others out, but really to keep themselves in so that they feel they do not have to change.

> Gabriel Archangel, with angels so white,
> raising our planet out of the dark night,
> as we now intone the Word of the Lord,
> the beings who fell are bound by your sword.
>
> **Gabriel Archangel, of this we are sure,**
> **Gabriel Archangel, Christ light is the cure.**
> **Gabriel Archangel, intentions so pure,**
> **Gabriel Archangel, in you we're secure.**

7. I call for the Christ light to challenge those who are trapped in the dualistic consciousness, who do not want to change, who do not want to look at themselves, who do not want to transcend.

Gabriel Archangel, we call now to you,
the astral plane your light burning through,
entities, demons, discarnates are bound,
as you and we intone Sacred Sound.

**Gabriel Archangel, of this we are sure,
Gabriel Archangel, Christ light is the cure.
Gabriel Archangel, intentions so pure,
Gabriel Archangel, in you we're secure.**

8. I invoke the awakening of the progressive people of America to the realization that we cannot transform anything outside of ourselves if we are not willing to transform ourselves.

Gabriel Archangel, what glorious day,
your radiant angels have come here to stay,
your purifications fire burning white,
intentions so pure, our hearts taking flight.

**Gabriel Archangel, of this we are sure,
Gabriel Archangel, Christ light is the cure.
Gabriel Archangel, intentions so pure,
Gabriel Archangel, in you we're secure.**

9. I invoke the awakening of the progressive people of America to the realization that, if we are true alchemists, we do not *find* the secret formula, we *become* the formula.

Gabriel Archangel, our planet so pure,
in our bright new future we do feel secure,
with your band of light encircling the earth,
Saint Germain's Golden Age is now given birth.

> Gabriel Archangel, of this we are sure,
> Gabriel Archangel, Christ light is the cure.
> Gabriel Archangel, intentions so pure,
> Gabriel Archangel, in you we're secure.

Part 4

1. I invoke the awakening of the progressive people of America to the realization that we become the open door for the light, and the light is what does the work and it cannot be forced by any matrix or structure on earth.

Serapis Bey, what power lies,
behind your purifying eyes.
Serapis Bey, it is a treat,
to enter your sublime retreat.

> Serapis Bey, we call to you,
> to help us dual lies see through,
> come purify our inner sight,
> we see the earth in your great light.

2. I invoke the awakening of the progressive people of America to the realization that the Holy Spirit bloweth where it listeth for it will always challenge the structure, whatever structure. It will compel those who are trapped in the structure to transcend and realize they are more than any structure.

> Serapis Bey, what wisdom found,
> your words are always most profound.
> Serapis Bey, we tell you true,
> our minds have room for naught but you.
>
> **Serapis Bey, we call to you,**
> **to help us dual lies see through,**
> **come purify our inner sight,**
> **we see the earth in your great light.**

3. I invoke the awakening of the progressive people of America to the realization that we are God-free spiritual beings with unlimited free will to define any self for ourselves that we are capable of and willing to imagine.

> Serapis Bey, what love beyond,
> our hearts do leap, as we respond.
> Serapis Bey, your life a poem,
> that calls us to our starry home.
>
> **Serapis Bey, we call to you,**
> **to help us dual lies see through,**
> **come purify our inner sight,**
> **we see the earth in your great light.**

4. I invoke the awakening of the progressive people of America to the realization that if we do not dare to imagine, then we cannot be alchemists.

> Serapis Bey, your guidance sure,
> our base is clear and white and pure.
> Serapis Bey, no longer trapped,
> by soul in which the self was wrapped.

> **Serapis Bey, we call to you,**
> **to help us dual lies see through,**
> **come purify our inner sight,**
> **we see the earth in your great light.**

5. I invoke the awakening of the progressive people of America to the realization that we cannot transcend that which is already manifest, if we dare not imagine anything beyond it, anything that is more.

> Serapis Bey, what healing balm,
> in mind that is forever calm.
> Serapis Bey, our thoughts are pure,
> your discipline we shall endure.

> **Serapis Bey, we call to you,**
> **to help us dual lies see through,**
> **come purify our inner sight,**
> **we see the earth in your great light.**

6. I invoke the awakening of the progressive people of America to the realization that becoming more does not mean becoming more than others or becoming more compared to any relative scale. It means transcending anything that already is.

> Serapis Bey, what secret test,
> for egos who want to be best.
> Serapis Bey, expose the "me,"
> that takes away our harmony.

> **Serapis Bey, we call to you,**
> **to help us dual lies see through,**
> **come purify our inner sight,**
> **we see the earth in your great light.**

7. I invoke the awakening of the progressive people of America to the realization that we cannot define some state of perfection, and think that when we have that perfection we no longer need to transcend.

> Serapis Bey, what moving sight,
> the self ascends to sacred height.
> Serapis Bey, forever free,
> in sacred synchronicity.

> **Serapis Bey, we call to you,**
> **to help us dual lies see through,**
> **come purify our inner sight,**
> **we see the earth in your great light.**

8. I invoke the awakening of the progressive people of America to the realization that Christ had to die on the cross. He had to give up the ghost before he could die and be reborn. There is no ultimate state on earth from which we do not have to transcend ourselves.

> Serapis Bey, you balance all,
> the seven rays upon our call.
> Serapis Bey, in space and time,
> the pyramid of self, we climb.

> Serapis Bey, we call to you,
> to help us dual lies see through,
> come purify our inner sight,
> we see the earth in your great light.

9. Serapis Bey, I am willing to go beyond understanding your teaching. I am willing to let it infuse my consciousness and accelerate me to the point where I can make that decision to accelerate to a higher level of consciousness.

> Serapis Bey, your Presence here,
> filling up the inner sphere.
> Life is now a sacred flow,
> God Purity we do bestow.

> Serapis Bey, we call to you,
> to help us dual lies see through,
> come purify our inner sight,
> we see the earth in your great light.

Sealing

In the name of the I AM THAT I AM, I accept that Archangel Michael, Astrea and Shiva form an impenetrable shield around myself and all constructive people, sealing us from all fear-based energies in all four octaves. I accept that the Light of God is consuming and transforming all fear-based energies that make up the dark forces working against America!

9 | THE PURPOSE OF DEMOCRACY IS NOT AFFLUENCE FOR ALL

This dictation was given at the National Archives Building, Washington, D.C.

Hilarion I AM. The Chohan of the Fifth Ray of higher vision. Thus, I am here to anchor the Flame of Higher Vision over this building of the National Archives, which houses some of the foundational documents of this nation, and thereby of the principles of modern democracy in its present form.

First and foremost, of course, there is the Declaration of Independence, signed by fifty courageous people who were willing to risk their lives and their earthly fortunes for the sake of manifesting a higher vision, a vision of a higher society, a higher form of government. Nevertheless, what could be brought forth at the time – in that fateful year, 1776 – was indeed only what could be brought forth given the level of humankind's collective awareness at that time. Thus, there is indeed relevance, as we have already said, in questioning the very foundations of modern democracy. As well as the omega aspect of how well modern democracy is actually functioning, in terms of doing what is said in the Declaration of Independence: securing the rights of the people.

Do democracies secure the rights of the people?

Are modern democratic governments truly securing the rights of the people? Or have they allowed themselves to become undermined or partially controlled by special interests, the interests of the few, the interests of the elite? There is a need for a debate. Is a democracy supposed to take care of the interests of the majority of the people, given their level of consciousness, so that a democracy at any time out-pictures the collective consciousness of a majority of the people? Or is a democracy supposed to challenge the majority to continually come up higher in consciousness so that both the people and the nation itself can manifest a higher state than what is currently manifest?

Of course, you see that when you are willing to fulfill the alpha requirement, there is no ultimate vision that is possible on earth. For as the collective consciousness is raised, and the level – the range of consciousness that is possible on earth – is therefore also raised, there is a need to reach for a still higher vision. You need to continue to do so on an indefinite basis, until the earth reaches the ascension point. Even then, of course, after the ascension point, there is continued growth.

9 | The purpose of democracy is not affluence for all

Is any truth self-evident to all people?

Take a look a this Declaration of Independence: "We hold these truths to be self-evident." Indeed, a bold statement when you consider the fact that there are 144 different levels of consciousness possible on earth. Is it realistic to say that a truth that seems self-evident at a certain level of consciousness will seem equally self-evident several levels of consciousness below?

Can those who are currently at, say, the 77th level of consciousness, can they really allow themselves to believe that those who are at the 5th level of consciousness will see as self-evident the truth that these people think is obvious? A new co-creator first comes into embodiment on earth at the 48th level of consciousness. This is the level where you have some sense that there is something beyond yourself, the self that you use to express yourself in the material realm.

At this point, you have not yet created a separate self. The choice is: Will you accelerate from where you start, and keep going up from the 48th level towards the 144th level, or will you choose to decelerate by going into the duality consciousness and the illusions of creating a separate self that can act without seeking attunement with your own higher self—or any higher vision or principles to guide you, but only letting yourself be guided by the fact that you define your own truth?

Do you not see that when you go into duality, you fulfill the prophecy given in the Book of Genesis? You have taken the forbidden fruit, so to speak, and you have now become as a "god" who knows good and evil, in the sense that you define what you think is good and evil based on your present level of consciousness. Can you not see that anyone who is below the 48th level of consciousness has defined his or her personal "truth," possibly by accepting a "truth" defined by the false leaders, namely the fallen beings in embodiment?

Nevertheless, each person has his or her personal vision of what is real and unreal. Therefore, when you speak a truth that seems self-evident from above the 48th level, well that truth will not seem self-evident to those who are below the 48th level. Thus indeed, the truth that is expressed in the Declaration of Independence was given from the 77th level of consciousness, quite a bit higher than the 48th level where new co-creators start.

Thus, is it not obvious that for anyone below the 48th level of consciousness, it will not be self-evident that all men are created equal? It will not be self-evident that all human beings are endowed by their Creator with unalienable rights; it will not be self-evident what those rights are. Indeed, those who are below the 48th level of consciousness may claim to believe in a god, but it is not a god that is transcendent; it is a god that is defined based on their own level of consciousness.

Rights based on a limited state of consciousness

It becomes obvious that even if you have the concept that people have rights, those rights must be defined by the "god" that you see from your level of consciousness. Therefore, the rights are surely an expression of your level of consciousness and what seems convenient to that level of consciousness. Therefore, it justifies why you do not have to transcend it, you do not have to challenge yourself by reaching for a higher vision than the closed mental box created by your current level

9 | The purpose of democracy is not affluence for all

of consciousness. When you are below the 48th level of consciousness, you think your mental box is closed, is complete, is infallible, has some higher authority. Thus, you do not need to question it. It is only when you go above the 48th level that you begin to see as self-evident that there will always be more to know, there will always be more to understand about life. Therefore, you can never really stop striving for that higher truth, that higher understanding, that higher vision that is indeed the driving force behind all life.

The Flame I am anchoring here is precisely that flame of accelerated vision that will challenge all of those who come to view these so-called sacred documents, to indeed question whether these documents reflect the highest possible vision and the highest possible foundation for a democracy. Therefore, they might be challenged to go within. Those who are beyond a certain level of consciousness, those who are beyond the 77th level at which the Declaration of Independence was given, they have the ability to begin to tune in to the higher vision. Which is indeed that all men were not created equal; they were created with equal rights to transcend their current state of consciousness. The deeper reality is that all self-aware beings were created unique, with a unique individuality. Their right is to expand that individuality, to transcend it, to accelerate it, to let it become MORE.

They, of course, also have a right to let it become less, by going below the 48th level and experience what it is like to be a separate self. Even this must, at least to some degree, be accepted by a free society. Yet it must, of course, also be accepted that these people should not be allowed to outplay their selfish tendencies, especially when those selfish tendencies are expressed as some form of altruism or some form of necessity for why the power elite should be allowed to rule. For can you not see, if you look at history, that there has never been a member of the power elite who had a level of consciousness above the 48th level? Indeed, then they could not act as an elite that was seeking to control and suppress the people. This would not be possible.

The key to a true democracy

I trust you can see that a true, functioning democracy must take into account that there are 144 levels. It must, therefore, seek to educate the population so that they can recognize what these levels are, and they can especially recognize people who are below the 48th level. Therefore, all can recognize the need to make sure that society cannot be controlled by those who are below that level of consciousness. They have a level of selfishness that will make them seek to manipulate a free society, to take advantage of the freedoms of a free society, in order to pursue what they see as some higher cause, even though it is simply a camouflaged form of self-interest.

There is indeed a need to write a constitution in such a way that there is a distinction made with reference to the levels of consciousness, and so that only those who are above a certain level of consciousness will be able to attain leading positions. This, of course, cannot be written into laws and constitutions unless it is recognized by the people. If it is recognized by the people, then it does not need to be written in great detail, for it is something that the people will be aware of and use for voting in those who are their leaders.

Of, course, as Gautama said yesterday in the Rotunda of the Capitol building, there is a need to let the people vote. Indeed, this will require a higher vision, for you cannot expect that the majority of the people would have a high level of consciousness that makes them able to see the self-evident truth of what is best for society. Thus, those who do have the higher level must indeed be very tolerant and very patient, and allow, sometimes, the majority to make decisions that will have undesirable consequences. Those who are above a certain level of consciousness can surely see what is coming, but they must step back sometimes and allow the people to act out their level of consciousness and reap the consequences. For this is how they learn and therefore become motivated to transcend.

It is only, truly, when you go beyond the 96th level – where the Christ begins to appear, and where the Christ Light and Christ Truth begins to become self-evident – well, it is only then that you fully transcend the need to have the second law of thermodynamics serve as your substitute teacher, by seeking to break down the structures in your mind and the structures in the world around you so that you are challenged to rethink your mental images. It is only when you reach that 96th level and beyond that you become self-driven in wanting to continually challenge your self-images and being truly willing to lock in to the Christ vision that enables you to challenge them. Of course, you cannot do this with reason, you cannot do this from the level of consciousness where you are at, as Lanto explained at the Jefferson Monument.

Indeed, this is the Flame that I have anchored during this dictation and will anchor as my messenger goes into the physical presence of these foundational documents. It is the flame that challenges all who come, all who come to Washington, D.C., to rethink their view of democracy and human rights and the purpose for human existence. For how can you have a functioning democracy if you do not have a sense of what is the purpose of human existence, namely the growth in self-awareness?

It is not the purpose of a democracy to create a free society with affluence for all. The welfare state is not the ultimate purpose of democracy. It is ultimate self-growth that is the purpose of democracy, and that requires self-government. This, of course, will be the topic of Nada, as she gives her address later. Thus, I will seal this release in the Flame that I AM – the Flame of accelerating, ever-accelerating, vision. Hilarion I AM.

10 | INVOKING A NEW VISION OF THE PURPOSE OF DEMOCRACY

In the name of the I AM THAT I AM, Jesus Christ, I use the authority that I have as a being in embodiment on earth to call upon Hilarion to reinforce my calls and use my chakras to project the statements in this invocation into the collective consciousness and awaken Americans to a new vision of the real purpose of democracy. Awaken Americans to the reality that we are spiritual beings and that we can co-create a new future by working with the ascended masters. I especially call for …

[Make your own calls here.]

Part 1

1. I invoke the Flame of Higher Vision that Hilarion has anchored over the building of the National Archives, which houses some of the foundational documents of this nation, and thereby of the principles of modern democracy in its present form.

> Cyclopea so dear, the truth you reveal,
> the truth that duality's ailments will heal,
> your Emerald Light is like a great balm,
> our emotional bodies are perfectly calm.

> **Cyclopea so dear, in Emerald Sphere,**
> **in raising perception we shall persevere,**
> **as deep in our hearts your truth we revere,**
> **to immaculate vision the earth does adhere.**

2. I invoke the awakening of the visionary people of America to the realization that what could be brought forth in 1776 was limited by the level of humankind's collective awareness at that time.

> Cyclopea so dear, with you we unwind,
> all negative spirals clouding the mind,
> we know pure awareness is truly our core,
> the key to becoming the wide-open door.

> **Cyclopea so dear, in Emerald Sphere,**
> **in raising perception we shall persevere,**
> **as deep in our hearts your truth we revere,**
> **to immaculate vision the earth does adhere.**

10 | Invoking a new vision of the purpose of democracy

3. I invoke the awakening of the visionary people of America to the realization that there is relevance in questioning the foundations of modern democracy.

> Cyclopea so dear, clear our inner sight,
> empowered, we pierce the soul's fearful night,
> we now see our life through your single eye,
> beyond all disease we're ready to fly.

> **Cyclopea so dear, in Emerald Sphere,**
> **in raising perception we shall persevere,**
> **as deep in our hearts your truth we revere,**
> **to immaculate vision the earth does adhere.**

4. I invoke the awakening of the visionary people of America to the realization that we need to question how well modern democracy is functioning, in terms of doing what is said in the Declaration of Independence: securing the rights of the people.

> Cyclopea so dear, life can only reflect,
> the images that the mind does project,
> the key to our healing is clearing the mind,
> from the images the ego is hiding behind.

> **Cyclopea so dear, in Emerald Sphere,**
> **in raising perception we shall persevere,**
> **as deep in our hearts your truth we revere,**
> **to immaculate vision the earth does adhere.**

5. I invoke the awakening of the visionary people of America to the realization that modern democratic governments are not truly securing the rights of the people because they have

allowed themselves to become undermined or partially controlled by special interests, the interests of the few, the interests of the elite.

> Cyclopea so dear, we want to aim high,
> to your healing flame we ever draw nigh,
> through veils of duality we now take flight,
> bathed in your penetrating Emerald Light.
>
> **Cyclopea so dear, in Emerald Sphere,**
> **in raising perception we shall persevere,**
> **as deep in our hearts your truth we revere,**
> **to immaculate vision the earth does adhere.**

6. I invoke the awakening of the visionary people of America to the realization that a democracy ideally should not be limited by the interests of the majority of the people, so that a democracy at any time out-pictures the collective consciousness of a majority of the people.

> Cyclopea so dear, your Emerald Flame,
> exposes every subtle, dualistic power game,
> including the game of wanting to say,
> that truth is defined in only one way.
>
> **Cyclopea so dear, in Emerald Sphere,**
> **in raising perception we shall persevere,**
> **as deep in our hearts your truth we revere,**
> **to immaculate vision the earth does adhere.**

7. I invoke the awakening of the visionary people of America to the realization that a democracy is supposed to challenge the majority to continually come up higher in consciousness, so

that both the people and the nation itself can manifest a higher state than what is currently manifest.

> Cyclopea so dear, we're feeling the flow,
> as your Living Truth upon us you bestow,
> from all dual vision we are now set free,
> planet earth in immaculate matrix will be.

> **Cyclopea so dear, in Emerald Sphere,**
> **in raising perception we shall persevere,**
> **as deep in our hearts your truth we revere,**
> **to immaculate vision the earth does adhere.**

8. I invoke the awakening of the visionary people of America to the realization that there is no ultimate vision that is possible on earth. As the collective consciousness is raised, there is a need to reach for a still higher vision.

> Cyclopea so dear, the truth is now clear,
> we see higher purpose for which we are here
> we know truth transcends all systems below,
> immersed in your light, we continue to grow.

> **Cyclopea so dear, in Emerald Sphere,**
> **in raising perception we shall persevere,**
> **as deep in our hearts your truth we revere,**
> **to immaculate vision the earth does adhere.**

9. I invoke the awakening of the visionary people of America to the realization that there are 144 different levels of consciousness possible on earth, and therefore no truth will be self-evident to all levels of consciousness.

Cyclopea so dear, we're feeling your joy,
as creative vision we now do employ,
in lifting earth out of serpentine cage,
to manifest Saint Germain's Golden Age.

**Cyclopea so dear, in Emerald Sphere,
in raising perception we shall persevere,
as deep in our hearts your truth we revere,
to immaculate vision the earth does adhere.**

Part 2

1. I invoke the awakening of the visionary people of America to the realization that what is self-evident to people at higher levels, will not be accepted by those who are blinded by the duality consciousness.

Raphael Archangel, your light so intense,
raise us beyond all human pretense.
Mother Mary and you have a vision so bold,
to see that our highest potential unfold.

**Raphael Archangel, for vision we pray,
Raphael Archangel, show us the way,
Raphael Archangel, your emerald ray,
Raphael Archangel, our lives a new day.**

2. I invoke the awakening of the visionary people of America to the realization that some people have taken the forbidden fruit, and they have become as a "god" who knows good and

evil, in the sense that they define good and evil based on their present level of consciousness.

> Raphael Archangel, in emerald sphere,
> to immaculate vision we always adhere.
> Mother Mary enfolds us in her Sacred Heart,
> from Mother's true love, we're never apart.

> **Raphael Archangel, for vision we pray,**
> **Raphael Archangel, show us the way,**
> **Raphael Archangel, your emerald ray,**
> **Raphael Archangel, our lives a new day.**

3. I invoke the awakening of the visionary people of America to the realization that anyone who is below the 48th level of consciousness has defined his or her personal truth, possibly by accepting a truth defined by the false leaders, namely the fallen beings.

> Raphael Archangel, all ailments you heal,
> each cell in our bodies in light now you seal.
> Mother Mary's immaculate concept we see,
> perfection of health our new reality.

> **Raphael Archangel, for vision we pray,**
> **Raphael Archangel, show us the way,**
> **Raphael Archangel, your emerald ray,**
> **Raphael Archangel, our lives a new day.**

4. I invoke the awakening of the visionary people of America to the realization that for anyone below the 48th level of consciousness, it will not be self-evident that all men are created equal. It will not be self-evident that all human beings are

endowed by their Creator with unalienable rights, and it will not be self-evident what those rights are.

> Raphael Archangel, your light is so real,
> the vision of Christ in us you reveal.
> Mother Mary now helps us to truly transcend,
> in emerald light with you we ascend.

> **Raphael Archangel, for vision we pray,**
> **Raphael Archangel, show us the way,**
> **Raphael Archangel, your emerald ray,**
> **Raphael Archangel, our lives a new day.**

5. I invoke the awakening of the visionary people of America to the realization that those who are below the 48th level of consciousness may claim to believe in a god, but it is not a god that is transcendent; it is a god that is defined based on their own level of consciousness.

> Raphael Archangel, diseases are done,
> as you help us see that all life is One,
> we no longer do your true love reject,
> immaculate vision on all we project.

> **Raphael Archangel, for vision we pray,**
> **Raphael Archangel, show us the way,**
> **Raphael Archangel, your emerald ray,**
> **Raphael Archangel, our lives a new day.**

6. I invoke the awakening of the visionary people of America to the realization that even if we have the concept that people have rights, those rights must be defined by the "god" that we see from our level of consciousness.

> Raphael Archangel, we're healing the earth,
> in immaculate vision we give her rebirth,
> a new era has on this day begun,
> your emerald light now shines like a sun.
>
> **Raphael Archangel, for vision we pray,**
> **Raphael Archangel, show us the way,**
> **Raphael Archangel, your emerald ray,**
> **Raphael Archangel, our lives a new day.**

7. I invoke the awakening of the visionary people of America to the realization that the rights are an expression of our level of consciousness and what seems convenient to that level of consciousness.

> Raphael Archangel, the fall is behind,
> as all of earth's people the Christ path do find,
> we call now to you all people to heal,
> as four lower bodies in love you do seal.
>
> **Raphael Archangel, for vision we pray,**
> **Raphael Archangel, show us the way,**
> **Raphael Archangel, your emerald ray,**
> **Raphael Archangel, our lives a new day.**

8. I invoke the awakening of the visionary people of America to the realization that this justifies why we do not have to transcend it, we do not have to challenge ourselves by reaching for a higher vision than the closed mental box created by our current level of consciousness.

Raphael Archangel, as you bring the light,
the forces of darkness swiftly take flight,
their day is now done as we claim the earth,
spreading to all an innocent mirth.

Raphael Archangel, for vision we pray,
Raphael Archangel, show us the way,
Raphael Archangel, your emerald ray,
Raphael Archangel, our lives a new day.

9. I invoke the awakening of the visionary people of America to the realization that when people are below the 48th level of consciousness, they think their mental box is closed, is complete, is infallible, has some higher authority. And thus, they do not need to question it.

Raphael Archangel, our vision set free,
as we can now see God's reality,
as Saint Germain's vision is manifest here,
the earth is now sealed in immaculate sphere.

Raphael Archangel, for vision we pray,
Raphael Archangel, show us the way,
Raphael Archangel, your emerald ray,
Raphael Archangel, our lives a new day.

Part 3

1. I invoke the awakening of the visionary people of America to the realization that it is only when we go above the 48th level that we begin to see as self-evident that there will always

10 | Invoking a new vision of the purpose of democracy

be more to know. Therefore, we can never stop striving for the higher vision that is the driving force behind all life.

> Hilarion, on emerald shore,
> we're free from all that's gone before.
> Hilarion, we let all go,
> that keeps us out of sacred flow.

> **Hilarion, with light so green,**
> **we see behind the matter screen,**
> **immaculate our inner sight,**
> **we see the earth is taking flight.**

2. I invoke the Flame of Accelerated Vision that will challenge those who come to view the sacred documents, so they will question whether these documents reflect the highest possible vision and the highest possible foundation for a democracy.

> Hilarion, the secret key,
> is wisdom's own reality.
> Hilarion, all life is healed,
> the ego's face no more concealed.

> **Hilarion, with light so green,**
> **we see behind the matter screen,**
> **immaculate our inner sight,**
> **we see the earth is taking flight.**

3. I invoke the awakening of the visionary people of America to the realization that a higher vision than the Declaration of Independence is that all men were not created equal; they were created with equal rights to transcend their current state of consciousness.

> Hilarion, your love for life,
> helps us surrender inner strife.
> Hilarion, your loving words,
> thrill our hearts like song of birds.
>
> **Hilarion, with light so green,**
> **we see behind the matter screen,**
> **immaculate our inner sight,**
> **we see the earth is taking flight.**

4. I invoke the awakening of the visionary people of America to the realization that all self-aware beings were created with a unique individuality. Our most basic right is to expand that individuality, to transcend it, to accelerate it, to let it become MORE.

> Hilarion, invoke the light,
> your sacred formulas recite.
> Hilarion, your secret tone,
> philosopher's most sacred stone.
>
> **Hilarion, with light so green,**
> **we see behind the matter screen,**
> **immaculate our inner sight,**
> **we see the earth is taking flight.**

5. I invoke the awakening of the visionary people of America to the realization that people also have a right to become less, by going below the 48th level and experience what it is like to be a separate self. Even this must be accepted by a free society.

10 | Invoking a new vision of the purpose of democracy

Hilarion, with love you greet,
us in your temple over Crete.
Hilarion, your emerald light,
the third eye sees with Christic sight.

**Hilarion, with light so green,
we see behind the matter screen,
immaculate our inner sight,
we see the earth is taking flight.**

6. I invoke the awakening of the visionary people of America to the realization that it must also be accepted that these people should not be allowed to outplay their selfish tendencies, especially when those selfish tendencies are expressed as some form of altruism or some form of necessity for why the power elite should be allowed to rule.

Hilarion, you give us fruit,
of truth that is so absolute.
Hilarion, all stress decrease,
as our ambitions we release.

**Hilarion, with light so green,
we see behind the matter screen,
immaculate our inner sight,
we see the earth is taking flight.**

7. I invoke the awakening of the visionary people of America to the realization that there has never been a member of the power elite who had a level of consciousness above the 48th level, for then they could not act as an elite that was seeking to control and suppress the people.

Hilarion, our chakras clear,
as we let go of subtlest fear.
Hilarion, we are sincere,
as freedom's truth we do revere.

Hilarion, with light so green,
we see behind the matter screen,
immaculate our inner sight,
we see the earth is taking flight.

8. I invoke the awakening of the visionary people of America to the realization that a true, functioning democracy must take into account that there are 144 levels. It must educate the population so they recognize people who are below the 48th level.

Hilarion, you balance all,
the seven rays upon our call.
Hilarion, you keep us true,
as we remain all one with you.

Hilarion, with light so green,
we see behind the matter screen,
immaculate our inner sight,
we see the earth is taking flight.

9. I invoke the awakening of the visionary people of America to the realization that we need to make sure that society cannot be controlled by those who have a level of selfishness that will make them seek to manipulate a free society.

> Hilarion, your Presence here,
> filling up the inner sphere.
> Life is now a sacred flow,
> God Vision we on all bestow.
>
> **Hilarion, with light so green,**
> **we see behind the matter screen,**
> **immaculate our inner sight,**
> **we see the earth is taking flight.**

Part 4

1. I invoke the awakening of the visionary people of America to the realization that the most selfish people will take advantage of the freedoms of a free society, in order to pursue what they see as some higher cause, even though it is simply a camouflaged form of self-interest.

> Hilarion, on emerald shore,
> we're free from all that's gone before.
> Hilarion, we let all go,
> that keeps us out of sacred flow.
>
> **Hilarion, with light so green,**
> **we see behind the matter screen,**
> **immaculate our inner sight,**
> **we see the earth is taking flight.**

2. I invoke the awakening of the visionary people of America to the realization that there is a need to write a constitution in such a way that there is a distinction made with reference to

the levels of consciousness, and so that only those who are above a certain level of consciousness will be able to attain leading positions.

> Hilarion, the secret key,
> is wisdom's own reality.
> Hilarion, all life is healed,
> the ego's face no more concealed.

> **Hilarion, with light so green,**
> **we see behind the matter screen,**
> **immaculate our inner sight,**
> **we see the earth is taking flight.**

3. I invoke the awakening of the visionary people of America to the realization that this cannot be written into laws and constitutions unless it is recognized by the people. If it is recognized by the people, then it does not need to be written in great detail, for it is something that the people will be aware of and use for voting in their leaders.

> Hilarion, your love for life,
> helps us surrender inner strife.
> Hilarion, your loving words,
> thrill our hearts like song of birds.

> **Hilarion, with light so green,**
> **we see behind the matter screen,**
> **immaculate our inner sight,**
> **we see the earth is taking flight.**

4. I invoke the awakening of the visionary people of America to the realization that there is a need to let the people vote.

10 | Invoking a new vision of the purpose of democracy

This will require a higher vision, for the majority might not have a high level of consciousness.

> Hilarion, invoke the light,
> your sacred formulas recite.
> Hilarion, your secret tone,
> philosopher's most sacred stone.

> **Hilarion, with light so green,**
> **we see behind the matter screen,**
> **immaculate our inner sight,**
> **we see the earth is taking flight.**

5. I invoke the awakening of the visionary people of America to the realization that those who do have the higher level of consciousness must be tolerant and patient, and allow the majority to make decisions that will have undesirable consequences.

> Hilarion, with love you greet,
> us in your temple over Crete.
> Hilarion, your emerald light,
> the third eye sees with Christic sight.

> **Hilarion, with light so green,**
> **we see behind the matter screen,**
> **immaculate our inner sight,**
> **we see the earth is taking flight.**

6. I invoke the awakening of the visionary people of America to the realization that those who are above a certain level of consciousness must step back and allow the people to act out their level of consciousness and reap the consequences.

For this is how they learn and therefore become motivated to transcend.

> Hilarion, you give us fruit,
> of truth that is so absolute.
> Hilarion, all stress decrease,
> as our ambitions we release.
>
> **Hilarion, with light so green,**
> **we see behind the matter screen,**
> **immaculate our inner sight,**
> **we see the earth is taking flight.**

7. I invoke the flame that challenges all who come to Washington, D.C. to rethink their view of democracy and human rights and the purpose for human existence. For how can we have a functioning democracy if we do not have a sense of what is the purpose of human existence, namely the growth in self-awareness?

> Hilarion, our chakras clear,
> as we let go of subtlest fear.
> Hilarion, we are sincere,
> as freedom's truth we do revere.
>
> **Hilarion, with light so green,**
> **we see behind the matter screen,**
> **immaculate our inner sight,**
> **we see the earth is taking flight.**

8. I invoke the awakening of the visionary people of America to the realization that it is not the purpose of a democracy to

create a free society with affluence for all. The welfare state is not the ultimate purpose of democracy.

> Hilarion, you balance all,
> the seven rays upon our call.
> Hilarion, you keep us true,
> as we remain all one with you.
>
> **Hilarion, with light so green,**
> **we see behind the matter screen,**
> **immaculate our inner sight,**
> **we see the earth is taking flight.**

9. I invoke the awakening of the visionary people of America to the realization that it is ultimate self-growth that is the purpose of democracy, and that requires self-government. For this purpose, I invoke the Flame of accelerating, ever-accelerating, vision from Hilarion.

> Hilarion, your Presence here,
> filling up the inner sphere.
> Life is now a sacred flow,
> God Vision we on all bestow.
>
> **Hilarion, with light so green,**
> **we see behind the matter screen,**
> **immaculate our inner sight,**
> **we see the earth is taking flight.**

Sealing

In the name of the I AM THAT I AM, I accept that Archangel Michael, Astrea and Shiva form an impenetrable shield around myself and all constructive people, sealing us from all fear-based energies in all four octaves. I accept that the Light of God is consuming and transforming all fear-based energies that make up the dark forces working against America!

11 | STAND UP TO THE ELITIST TENDENCIES IN GOVERNMENT

This dictation was given in front of the United States Capitol Building in Washington, D.C.

Nada I AM, the Chohan of the Sixth Ray. Ministration and service. Peace. But even the higher vision of the beginning of the integration of the knowledge that you are part of a whole that is greater than yourself and any other part of the whole. For truly, the whole is more than the sum of the parts—when a critical mass of the self-aware beings who are part of the whole are willing to acknowledge that they are more than the lower self, more than the separate self.

This, of course, is the critical ingredient to make this Capitol building, and the government that resides within it, work. Will these representatives recognize that they each are more—more than their personal selves, more than the special interests that are impinging upon them from all sides through the lobbying groups or the bureaucracy, or even more than the people they represent in their home states? Truly, is there any one state in this Union that can dominate the Union? Is it not so that the Union is more than the sum of the states? If there is not this awareness, then how can the Union function, how can the government function?

The veils of secrecy will come down

Thus, I come to anchor here the Flame of the Sixth Ray, throughout this entire building, as the omega supplement to Gautama Buddha's Presence in the rotunda. This Flame will go out into every nook and cranny of this building, above and below ground. It will penetrate all aspects of the American government, even those that they think they have hidden from the people, under some justification, so to speak, of secrecy.

There is nothing secret for the Chohan of the Sixth Ray. For I have been involved in God government for a long time and I know how to look through even the most hidden compartments of human government. You think you can hide from the ascended masters? You can hide nothing! There is nothing hidden that shall not be revealed, as stated by Jesus, the foremost representative of the Sixth Ray to embody in known history.

Thus, I predict indeed, after the anchoring of this Flame, you will begin to see the unveiling of all the secrets that they think they can keep hidden from the people. This Flame will challenge those veils of secrecy. As indeed, Gautama Buddha said at New Year's, how they will start coming down, and how you will see that the Mother itself will spew out of her womb those who think they can stay in there longer than their allotted time. Those who think they can hide in the womb, and thus not having to transcend themselves and their comfortability.

"Let it all hang out," as they say. For you can no longer hang out in the mother's womb, if you are not willing to work for raising the all of the entire cosmos that resides in the Mother's greater womb. You may think you can create your own little compartment, set apart from the whole. You cannot, for these separate compartments will begin to crumble around you, and the walls of secrecy will come down. Let this be a word of warning to those in this building, who think they can hide from their own people how they are pursuing the interests of special groups, of elite groups, who have the money to finance the lobbying groups or buy favors. This will not be allowed to stand anymore, as the people will not tolerate it and will demand openness. They will demand the service of the All.

The two main failures of Congress

The two most spectacular failures of the Congress and the Senate to fulfill their mission, in recent times, has indeed been that they failed to stand up to President Bush when he presented the false evidence that seemingly, at the time, justified the invasion of Iraq. The second incident was when they also failed to stand up to President Bush and the bailout of the big investment banks on Wall Street.

In both cases, neither the Senate nor Congress were willing to fulfill their role of balancing the President, making sure that the President would not go on some ego trip, mislead by special interest groups. This is their true role in the constitutional system: To make sure that no branch of government can go too far. They failed spectacularly on both occasions, and this is what needs to be seen by the people so that they demand that this will not happen again.

There is indeed a need to rethink this government and make sure it is *of* the people, *by* the people and *for* the people. Of course, it is necessary to go many steps up towards that ultimate goal of self-government. Is the American nation a self-governing nation? Do the American people govern themselves or have they allowed their so-called elected representatives to form an elite that is not governing based on what is the will of the people? How can it be that this institution – which is meant to represent one nation under God, indivisible, with liberty and justice for all – is still divided between Republicans and Democrats, and now adding the discordant voices of the Tea Party?

How can it be that they have not voluntarily transcended this dualistic system and realized that it is not viable to have this institution constantly ping–ponging between the extremes, of the extreme Democratic position and the extreme Republican position. When in reality the majority of the people are squarely in the center of American politics, doing the best they can according to their state of consciousness to pursue the Middle Way—that is not in-between the extremes, but transcends the extremes based on a higher vision.

This is not the will of the people, nor is it the will of the Founding Fathers. I challenge all of the elected representatives, the media, the bureaucracy, and the people themselves to openly acknowledge this. Therefore, to look at this building and say: "But the Emperor has nothing on." The senators and congressmen who claim to represent the will of the people but have sold out to special interests—they have nothing on. Even if they believe they are serving some greater cause or just plain reality politics, they still have nothing on.

Thus, it is time to say: "Gridlock be gone! You have no power in this house of the people. We do not want gridlock. We want you to lock in to the grid of the ascended masters and the grid of Saint Germain for the matrix for the Golden Age in America." This is the grid you need to lock in to. Not your own, self-created grid, based on your dualistic state of consciousness that you are not willing to transcend for the good of the Union.

The challenge to transcend gridlock

I AM a female ascended master, yet I can – and I *will* when necessary – embody the wrath of Kali. This is indeed the wrath of Kali, challenging you to overcome your gridlock that is the gridlock in your own state of consciousness—for you will not transcend the mental box you have created and in which you are comfortable. Get beyond it, NOW! Or go down with it, as it is taken down by the second law of thermodynamics and the will of the people. For this shall not stand, this abomination of desolation shall not stand in this, what should be the holy place of this democratic nation.

Take heed then, or you will see that your own people will rise up against you, not in an unsimilar manner as to what you have seen in Tunisia and Egypt recently, and that you are likely to see in other nations in coming years. As indeed, those who are the representatives of the Mother will take a stand against those who should be representing the Father but are not. For they are not willing to lock in to the higher vision of service and be the instruments of peace.

Was it indeed serving the cause of peace to allow the President to go on, what was essentially an ego trip of a small elite of neo-conservatives, in order to get this nation to go to war? You, the Congress and the Senate, should be representing the Sixth Ray. Therefore, you should heed the words of Christ: "Judge not after the appearance but judge righteous judgment." When you allowed the President to, so to speak, "convince" you to back his invasion of Iraq based on not only appearances as observed, but appearances as manufactured, you compromised your mission and your authority given to you by the people.

You violated the sacred principle of "the consent of the governed," because you did not have the consent of the governed. Some of the senators and congressmen allowed themselves to be intimidated by this appearance of patriotism and loyalty. As did many among the people who thought they had to support the President going to war in order to be patriotic and loyal. But you are not loyal if you are not willing to exercise discernment. For you cannot go to war under the pretext of serving a greater cause – and indeed be serving the cause of the power elite – and then at the same time maintain your sponsorship from Saint Germain. This simply is not a realistic expectation, and thus you, the people, must stand up to your own government when they do something that you know in your hearts is not right and is not what you want to see for this nation.

How many more pointless wars?

How many times do we need to see this American government become involved with these pointless wars? Can you not see that even President Obama, who came to power based on an agenda of promoting change, was, from the very beginning, hampered by the previous administration's bailout of the financial world and their engagement in Iraq and Afghanistan? He made the momentous mistake of judgment, of judging after the appearance, believing his advisors that he could win some decisive victory in Afghanistan by committing more troops and money.

There is no decisive victory to be won in Afghanistan or anywhere else. You cannot force a people to be free until they are ready, as proven by the fact that the Egyptian people could not stand up to their own dictator until after 30 years of brutal repression. Now, that they have stood up and overturned the dictator, what will they do next? How will they avoid going into a period of chaos and turmoil when indeed the dictator prevented them from ever developing any kind of organization that was ready to take over government after the dictator?

It is guaranteed that there will be a vacuum, and in a vacuum there is usually chaos until there is rebirth and a new order emerges. Hold the vision that this will not be a "new world order" based on the vision of the power elite, but that it will be a new matrix based on the golden age vision of Saint Germain for both Egypt and other nations, and this nation of the United States.

Sometimes it is indeed better that there be chaos than the continued stillstand. Yes, you might even see chaos in these United States where you think everything is under control. The power elite think everything is under control, but they will see that control begin to crumble when the very people they trust to exercise the control will refuse to do so in greater numbers and with greater boldness. Thus, I have anchored the flame, the Flame of the Sixth Ray, the accelerated peace of oneness, of coming into unity based on a greater sense, a greater vision, of the whole. Thus, my release is complete, I seal it. Nada I AM.

12 | INVOKING AN END TO THE ELITIST TENDENCIES IN GOVERNMENT

In the name of the I AM THAT I AM, Jesus Christ, I use the authority that I have as a being in embodiment on earth to call upon Nada to reinforce my calls and use my chakras to project the statements in this invocation into the collective consciousness and awaken Americans to the need to rise above elitist tendencies in the government. Awaken Americans to the reality that we are spiritual beings and that we can co-create a new future by working with the ascended masters. I especially call for …

[Make your own calls here.]

Part 1

1. I invoke the awakening of the peace-loving people of America to the knowledge that we are part of a whole that is greater than ourselves and we are connected to any other part of the whole.

> O Elohim Peace, in Unity's Flame,
> there is no more room for duality's game,
> we know that all form is from the same source,
> empowering us to plot a new course.
>
> **O Elohim Peace, through your tranquility,**
> **we are free from the chaos of duality,**
> **in oneness with God a new identity,**
> **we are raising the earth into Infinity.**

2. I invoke the awakening of the peace-loving people of America to the realization that the whole is more than the sum of the parts—when a critical mass of the self-aware beings who are part of the whole are willing to acknowledge that we are more than the separate self.

> O Elohim Peace, the bell now you ring,
> causing all atoms to vibrate and sing,
> we give up the sense of a separate "me,"
> we're crossing Samsara's turbulent sea.
>
> **O Elohim Peace, through your tranquility,**
> **we are free from the chaos of duality,**
> **in oneness with God a new identity,**
> **we are raising the earth into Infinity.**

12 | Invoking an end to the elitist tendencies in government

3. I invoke the awakening of the peace-loving people of America to the realization that this is the critical ingredient to make this Capitol building work and to make the government that resides within it work.

> O Elohim Peace, you help us to know,
> that Jesus has come your Flame to bestow,
> upon all who are ready to give up the strife,
> by following Christ into infinite life.
>
> **O Elohim Peace, through your tranquility,**
> **we are free from the chaos of duality,**
> **in oneness with God a new identity,**
> **we are raising the earth into Infinity.**

4. I invoke the awakening of the peace-loving people of America to the realization that the representatives need to recognize that they each are more—more than their personal selves, more than the special interests that are impinging upon them from all sides through the lobbying groups or the bureaucracy, or even more than the people they represent in their home states.

> O Elohim Peace, through your eyes we see,
> that only in oneness will we ever be free,
> we now see that there is no separate thing,
> to the ego-based self we no longer cling.
>
> **O Elohim Peace, through your tranquility,**
> **we are free from the chaos of duality,**
> **in oneness with God a new identity,**
> **we are raising the earth into Infinity.**

5. I invoke the awakening of the peace-loving people of America to the realization that no one state in this Union can dominate the Union, for the Union is more than the sum of the states.

> O Elohim Peace, you show us the way,
> for clearing the mind from duality's fray,
> you pierce the illusions of both time and space,
> separation consumed by your Infinite Grace.

> **O Elohim Peace, through your tranquility,**
> **we are free from the chaos of duality,**
> **in oneness with God a new identity,**
> **we are raising the earth into Infinity.**

6. I invoke the awakening of the peace-loving people of America to the realization that if there is not this awareness, then the Union cannot function, the government cannot function.

> O Elohim Peace, what beauty your name,
> consuming within us duality's shame,
> the earth is set free from burden of fear,
> accepting your peace is now manifest here.

> **O Elohim Peace, through your tranquility,**
> **we are free from the chaos of duality,**
> **in oneness with God a new identity,**
> **we are raising the earth into Infinity.**

7. I invoke the Flame of the Sixth Ray, anchored by Nada throughout this entire building, as the Omega supplement to Gautama Buddha's presence in the rotunda.

O Elohim Peace, with Christ at our side,
no force of duality can evermore hide,
It was through the vibration of your Golden Flame,
that Christ the illusion of death overcame.

O Elohim Peace, through your tranquility,
we are free from the chaos of duality,
in oneness with God a new identity,
we are raising the earth into Infinity.

8. I call for this Flame to go into every nook and cranny of this Capitol building, above and below ground. I call for it to penetrate all aspects of the American government, even those that they think they have hidden from the people, under some justification of secrecy.

O Elohim Peace, you bring now to earth,
the unstoppable flame of Cosmic Rebirth,
we give up the sense that something is "mine,"
allowing your Light through our beings to shine.

O Elohim Peace, through your tranquility,
we are free from the chaos of duality,
in oneness with God a new identity,
we are raising the earth into Infinity.

9. I invoke the awakening of the peace-loving people of America to the realization that we can hide nothing from the ascended masters. I demand that everything that is hidden shall be revealed, and I invoke the momentum of Jesus to expose all that is not of Christ in this Capitol building.

> O Elohim Peace, as peace now we feel,
> all records of war you totally heal,
> the earth is now free from forces of war,
> restoring her purity known from before.
>
> **O Elohim Peace, through your tranquility,**
> **we are free from the chaos of duality,**
> **in oneness with God a new identity,**
> **we are raising the earth into Infinity.**

Part 2

1. I call for the unveiling of all the secrets that they think they can keep hidden from the people. I call for the Flame to challenge those veils of secrecy.

> O Elohim Peace, in Unity's Flame,
> there is no more room for duality's game,
> we know that all form is from the same source,
> empowering us to plot a new course.
>
> **O Elohim Peace, through your tranquility,**
> **we are free from the chaos of duality,**
> **in oneness with God a new identity,**
> **we are raising the earth into Infinity.**

2. I call for the Mother itself to spew out of her womb those who think they can stay in there longer than their allotted time, those who think they can hide in the womb, and thus not having to transcend themselves and their comfortability.

12 | Invoking an end to the elitist tendencies in government

O Elohim Peace, the bell now you ring,
causing all atoms to vibrate and sing,
we give up the sense of a separate "me,"
we're crossing Samsara's turbulent sea.

**O Elohim Peace, through your tranquility,
we are free from the chaos of duality,
in oneness with God a new identity,
we are raising the earth into Infinity.**

3. I invoke the judgment of Christ upon those who are not willing to work for raising the All of the entire cosmos that resides in the Mother's greater womb.

O Elohim Peace, you help us to know,
that Jesus has come your Flame to bestow,
upon all who are ready to give up the strife,
by following Christ into infinite life.

**O Elohim Peace, through your tranquility,
we are free from the chaos of duality,
in oneness with God a new identity,
we are raising the earth into Infinity.**

4. I invoke the judgment of Christ upon those who think they can create their own little compartment, set apart from the whole. I call for these separate compartments to crumble and the walls of secrecy to come down.

O Elohim Peace, through your eyes we see,
that only in oneness will we ever be free,
we now see that there is no separate thing,
to the ego-based self we no longer cling.

> **O Elohim Peace, through your tranquility,**
> **we are free from the chaos of duality,**
> **in oneness with God a new identity,**
> **we are raising the earth into Infinity.**

5. I call forth the judgment of Christ upon those in this Capitol building who think they can hide from their own people how they are pursuing the interests of special groups, of elite groups, who have the money to finance the lobbying groups or buy favors.

> O Elohim Peace, you show us the way,
> for clearing the mind from duality's fray,
> you pierce the illusions of both time and space,
> separation consumed by your Infinite Grace.

> **O Elohim Peace, through your tranquility,**
> **we are free from the chaos of duality,**
> **in oneness with God a new identity,**
> **we are raising the earth into Infinity.**

6. I invoke the awakening of the peace-loving people of America to the realization that this will not be allowed to stand anymore, as we will not tolerate it and we demand openness. We demand the service of the All.

> O Elohim Peace, what beauty your name,
> consuming within us duality's shame,
> the earth is set free from burden of fear,
> accepting your peace is now manifest here.

> **O Elohim Peace, through your tranquility,**
> **we are free from the chaos of duality,**
> **in oneness with God a new identity,**
> **we are raising the earth into Infinity.**

7. I invoke the awakening of the peace-loving people of America to the realization that the role of the Senate and Congress is to balance the President, making sure that the President does not go on some ego trip, mislead by special interest groups.

> O Elohim Peace, with Christ at our side,
> no force of duality can evermore hide,
> It was through the vibration of your Golden Flame,
> that Christ the illusion of death overcame.

> **O Elohim Peace, through your tranquility,**
> **we are free from the chaos of duality,**
> **in oneness with God a new identity,**
> **we are raising the earth into Infinity.**

8. I invoke the awakening of the peace-loving people of America to the realization that the role of the Senate and Congress in the constitutional system is to make sure that no branch of government can go too far.

> O Elohim Peace, you bring now to earth,
> the unstoppable flame of Cosmic Rebirth,
> we give up the sense that something is "mine,"
> allowing your Light through our beings to shine.

> **O Elohim Peace, through your tranquility,**
> **we are free from the chaos of duality,**
> **in oneness with God a new identity,**
> **we are raising the earth into Infinity.**

9. I invoke the awakening of the peace-loving people of America to the realization that there is a need to rethink this government and make sure it is *of* the people, *by* the people and *for* the people.

> O Elohim Peace, as peace now we feel,
> all records of war you totally heal,
> the earth is now free from forces of war,
> restoring her purity known from before.

> **O Elohim Peace, through your tranquility,**
> **we are free from the chaos of duality,**
> **in oneness with God a new identity,**
> **we are raising the earth into Infinity.**

Part 3

1. I invoke the awakening of the peace-loving people of America to the realization that it is necessary to go many steps up towards that ultimate goal of self-government.

> Uriel Archangel, immense is the power,
> of angels of peace, all war to devour.
> The demons of war, no match for your light,
> consuming them all, with radiance so bright.

12 | Invoking an end to the elitist tendencies in government

> **Uriel Archangel, use your great sword,**
> **Uriel Archangel, consume all discord,**
> **Uriel Archangel, we're of one accord,**
> **Uriel Archangel, we walk with the Lord.**

2. I invoke the awakening of the peace-loving people of America to the realization that we need to ask if the American nation is a self-governing nation? Do the American people govern themselves, or have we allowed our so-called elected representatives to form an elite that is not governing based on the will of the people?

> Uriel Archangel, intense is the sound,
> when millions of angels, their voices compound.
> They build a crescendo, piercing the night,
> life's glorious oneness revealed to our sight.

> **Uriel Archangel, use your great sword,**
> **Uriel Archangel, consume all discord,**
> **Uriel Archangel, we're of one accord,**
> **Uriel Archangel, we walk with the Lord.**

3. I invoke the awakening of the peace-loving people of America to the realization that we need to ask how it can be that this institution – which is meant to represent "One Nation under God, indivisible, with liberty and justice for all" – is still divided between Republicans and Democrats?

> Uriel Archangel, from out the Great Throne,
> your millions of trumpets, sound the One Tone.
> Consuming all discord with your harmony,
> the sound of all sounds will set all life free.

**Uriel Archangel, use your great sword,
Uriel Archangel, consume all discord,
Uriel Archangel, we're of one accord,
Uriel Archangel, we walk with the Lord.**

4. I invoke the awakening of the peace-loving people of America to the realization that we need to ask why we have not voluntarily transcended this dualistic system and realized that it is not viable to have this institution constantly ping–ponging between the extreme Democratic position and the extreme Republican position.

Uriel Archangel, all war is now done,
for you bring a message, from heart of the One.
The hearts of all men, now singing in peace,
the spirals of love, forever increase.

**Uriel Archangel, use your great sword,
Uriel Archangel, consume all discord,
Uriel Archangel, we're of one accord,
Uriel Archangel, we walk with the Lord.**

5. I invoke the awakening of the peace-loving people of America to the realization that the majority of the people are squarely in the center of American politics, doing the best they can according to their state of consciousness to pursue the Middle Way — that is not in-between the extremes, but transcends the extremes based on a higher vision.

Uriel Archangel, your infinite peace,
from all warring beings our planet release,
war is a prison from which we are free,
embracing the peace of true unity.

12 | Invoking an end to the elitist tendencies in government

Uriel Archangel, use your great sword,
Uriel Archangel, consume all discord,
Uriel Archangel, we're of one accord,
Uriel Archangel, we walk with the Lord.

6. I invoke the awakening of the peace-loving people of America to the realization that the polarization of Congress is not the will of the people, nor is it the will of the Founding Fathers. I challenge all of the elected representatives, the media, the bureaucracy, and the people themselves to openly acknowledge this.

Uriel Archangel, we send forth the call,
reveal now the oneness that unifies all,
help us the vision of peace now to see,
so we from all conflicts and struggles are free.

Uriel Archangel, use your great sword,
Uriel Archangel, consume all discord,
Uriel Archangel, we're of one accord,
Uriel Archangel, we walk with the Lord.

7. I invoke the awakening of the peace-loving people of America to the realization that we need to look at this building and say: "But the Emperor has nothing on." The senators and congressmen who claim to represent the will of the people but have sold out to special interests—they have nothing on.

Uriel Archangel, in service to life,
you give us release from struggle and strife,
forgetting the self is truly the key,
to living a life in true harmony.

**Uriel Archangel, use your great sword,
Uriel Archangel, consume all discord,
Uriel Archangel, we're of one accord,
Uriel Archangel, we walk with the Lord.**

8. I invoke the awakening of the peace-loving people of America to the realization that it is time to say: "Gridlock be gone! You have no power in this house of the people. We do not want gridlock. We want you to lock in to the grid of the ascended masters and the grid of Saint Germain for the matrix of the Golden Age in America."

Uriel Archangel, the earth now you raise,
out of duality's death-bringing haze,
we call now upon your great Flame of Peace,
commanding that all petty squabbles do cease.

**Uriel Archangel, use your great sword,
Uriel Archangel, consume all discord,
Uriel Archangel, we're of one accord,
Uriel Archangel, we walk with the Lord.**

9. I invoke the awakening of the peace-loving people of America to the realization that this is the grid we need to lock in to. Not our own, self-created grid, based on our dualistic state of consciousness that we are not willing to transcend for the good of the Union.

Uriel Archangel, as peace is the norm,
to your higher vision the earth does conform,
as people have found your peace from within,
a Golden Age is the prize that we win.

**Uriel Archangel, use your great sword,
Uriel Archangel, consume all discord,
Uriel Archangel, we're of one accord,
Uriel Archangel, we walk with the Lord.**

Part 4

1. I invoke the awakening of the peace-loving people of America to the realization that we need to challenge our representatives to overcome the gridlock that is the gridlock in their own state of consciousness—for they will not transcend the mental box they have created and in which they are comfortable.

Uriel Archangel, immense is the power,
of angels of peace, all war to devour.
The demons of war, no match for your light,
consuming them all, with radiance so bright.

**Uriel Archangel, use your great sword,
Uriel Archangel, consume all discord,
Uriel Archangel, we're of one accord,
Uriel Archangel, we walk with the Lord.**

2. I invoke the awakening of the peace-loving people of America to the realization that we all need to go beyond our mental box or go down with it, as it is taken down by the second law of thermodynamics and the will of the people.

> Uriel Archangel, intense is the sound,
> when millions of angels, their voices compound.
> They build a crescendo, piercing the night,
> life's glorious oneness revealed to our sight.
>
> **Uriel Archangel, use your great sword,**
> **Uriel Archangel, consume all discord,**
> **Uriel Archangel, we're of one accord,**
> **Uriel Archangel, we walk with the Lord.**

3. I invoke the awakening of the peace-loving people of America to say: "This shall not stand, this abomination of desolation shall not stand in this, what should be the holy place of this democratic nation."

> Uriel Archangel, from out the Great Throne,
> your millions of trumpets, sound the One Tone.
> Consuming all discord with your harmony,
> the sound of all sounds will set all life free.
>
> **Uriel Archangel, use your great sword,**
> **Uriel Archangel, consume all discord,**
> **Uriel Archangel, we're of one accord,**
> **Uriel Archangel, we walk with the Lord.**

4. I invoke the awakening of the peace-loving people of America to the realization that those who are the representatives of the Mother must take a stand against those who should be representing the Father but are not. For they are not willing to lock in to the higher vision of service and be the instruments of peace.

12 | Invoking an end to the elitist tendencies in government

> Uriel Archangel, all war is now done,
> for you bring a message, from heart of the One.
> The hearts of all men, now singing in peace,
> the spirals of love, forever increase.
>
> **Uriel Archangel, use your great sword,**
> **Uriel Archangel, consume all discord,**
> **Uriel Archangel, we're of one accord,**
> **Uriel Archangel, we walk with the Lord.**

5. I invoke the awakening of the peace-loving people of America to the realization that the Congress and the Senate should be representing peace and should heed the words of Christ: "Judge not after the appearance but judge righteous judgment."

> Uriel Archangel, your infinite peace,
> from all warring beings our planet release,
> war is a prison from which we are free,
> embracing the peace of true unity.
>
> **Uriel Archangel, use your great sword,**
> **Uriel Archangel, consume all discord,**
> **Uriel Archangel, we're of one accord,**
> **Uriel Archangel, we walk with the Lord.**

6. I invoke the awakening of the peace-loving people of America to the realization that we need to invoke the sacred principle of "the consent of the governed" so that our nation will never again go to war based on manipulated appearances.

> Uriel Archangel, we send forth the call,
> reveal now the oneness that unifies all,
> help us the vision of peace now to see,
> so we from all conflicts and struggles are free.
>
> **Uriel Archangel, use your great sword,**
> **Uriel Archangel, consume all discord,**
> **Uriel Archangel, we're of one accord,**
> **Uriel Archangel, we walk with the Lord.**

7. I invoke the awakening of the peace-loving people of America to the realization that we cannot allow ourselves to be intimidated by this appearance of patriotism and loyalty where we think we have to support the President going to war in order to be patriotic and loyal.

> Uriel Archangel, in service to life,
> you give us release from struggle and strife,
> forgetting the self is truly the key,
> to living a life in true harmony.
>
> **Uriel Archangel, use your great sword,**
> **Uriel Archangel, consume all discord,**
> **Uriel Archangel, we're of one accord,**
> **Uriel Archangel, we walk with the Lord.**

8. I invoke the awakening of the peace-loving people of America to the realization that we are not loyal if we are not willing to exercise discernment.

12 | Invoking an end to the elitist tendencies in government

> Uriel Archangel, the earth now you raise,
> out of duality's death-bringing haze,
> we call now upon your great Flame of Peace,
> commanding that all petty squabbles do cease.
>
> **Uriel Archangel, use your great sword,**
> **Uriel Archangel, consume all discord,**
> **Uriel Archangel, we're of one accord,**
> **Uriel Archangel, we walk with the Lord.**

9. I invoke the awakening of the peace-loving people of America to the realization that we cannot go to war under the pretext of serving a greater cause, which is serving the cause of the power elite, and then at the same time maintain our sponsorship from Saint Germain.

> Uriel Archangel, as peace is the norm,
> to your higher vision the earth does conform,
> as people have found your peace from within,
> a Golden Age is the prize that we win.
>
> **Uriel Archangel, use your great sword,**
> **Uriel Archangel, consume all discord,**
> **Uriel Archangel, we're of one accord,**
> **Uriel Archangel, we walk with the Lord.**

Part 5

1. I invoke the awakening of the peace-loving people of America to the realization that we, the people, must stand up to our own government when they do something that we know in

our hearts is not right and is not what we want to see for this nation.

> Master Nada, beauty's power,
> unfolding like a sacred flower.
> Master Nada, so sublime,
> a will that conquers even time.
>
> **Master Nada, peace you give,**
> **forevermore in peace we live,**
> **our planet has a peaceful morn,**
> **the Golden Age is hereby born.**

2. I invoke the awakening of the peace-loving people of America to the realization that we must demand that the American government never again becomes involved with these pointless wars.

> Master Nada, you bestow,
> upon us wisdom's rushing flow.
> Master Nada, mind so strong
> rising on your wings of song.
>
> **Master Nada, peace you give,**
> **forevermore in peace we live,**
> **our planet has a peaceful morn,**
> **the Golden Age is hereby born.**

3. I invoke the awakening of the peace-loving people of America to the realization that we need to demand that our government awakens from the illusion that we could win some decisive victory by committing more troops and money.

12 | *Invoking an end to the elitist tendencies in government*

Master Nada, precious scent,
your love is truly heaven-sent.
Master Nada, kind and soft
on wings of love we rise aloft.

**Master Nada, peace you give,
forevermore in peace we live,
our planet has a peaceful morn,
the Golden Age is hereby born.**

4. I invoke the awakening of the peace-loving people of America to the realization that there is no decisive victory to be won anywhere, for we cannot force people to be free until they are ready.

Master Nada, mother light,
our hearts are rising like a kite.
Master Nada, from your view,
all life is pure as morning dew.

**Master Nada, peace you give,
forevermore in peace we live,
our planet has a peaceful morn,
the Golden Age is hereby born.**

5. I invoke the awakening of the peace-loving people of America to the realization that we must hold the vision that there will not be a "new world order" based on the vision of the power elite, but that there will be a new matrix based on the golden-age vision of Saint Germain.

Master Nada, truth you bring,
as morning birds in love do sing.
Master Nada, we now feel,
your love that all four bodies heal.

**Master Nada, peace you give,
forevermore in peace we live,
our planet has a peaceful morn,
the Golden Age is hereby born.**

6. I invoke the awakening of the peace-loving people of America to the realization that sometimes it is better that there be chaos than the continued stillstand.

Master Nada, serve in peace,
as all emotions we release.
Master Nada, life is fun,
the solar plexus is a sun.

**Master Nada, peace you give,
forevermore in peace we live,
our planet has a peaceful morn,
the Golden Age is hereby born.**

7. I invoke the awakening of the peace-loving people of America to the realization that we must be willing to see chaos in these United States, for it is necessary that the control of the power elite begins to crumble.

Master Nada, love is free,
conditions we no longer see.
Master Nada, rise above,
all human forms of lesser love.

**Master Nada, peace you give,
forevermore in peace we live,
our planet has a peaceful morn,
the Golden Age is hereby born.**

8. I call for the cutting free of the people that the power elite trust to exercise their control, so they will refuse to do so in greater numbers and with greater boldness.

Master Nada, balance all,
the seven rays upon our call.
Master Nada, rise and shine,
your radiant beauty most divine.

**Master Nada, peace you give,
forevermore in peace we live,
our planet has a peaceful morn,
the Golden Age is hereby born.**

9. I invoke the Flame of the Sixth Ray, the accelerated peace of oneness, of coming into unity based on a greater sense, a greater vision, of the whole. I call for this Flame to penetrate this Capitol Building of the United States of America and to awaken those who will be awakened and to judge those who will not be awakened.

Nada Dear, your Presence here,
filling up the inner sphere.
Life is now a sacred flow,
God Peace we do on all bestow.

**Master Nada, peace you give,
forevermore in peace we live,
our planet has a peaceful morn,
the Golden Age is hereby born.**

Sealing

In the name of the I AM THAT I AM, I accept that Archangel Michael, Astrea and Shiva form an impenetrable shield around myself and all constructive people, sealing us from all fear-based energies in all four octaves. I accept that the Light of God is consuming and transforming all fear-based energies that make up the dark forces working against America!

13 | THE NEED TO TRANSCEND REPRESENTATIVE DEMOCRACY

This dictation was given in the Rotunda of the U.S. Capitol building, Washington, D.C.

Gautama Buddha is the name I have used now in connection with my service on this earth. I am taking this opportunity – as I have a messenger who is in physical embodiment, and who is in this physical location in the Rotunda of the United States Capitol – to anchor a greater amount of my Presence than I have anchored here earlier, a greater intensity of the Light that I AM, the Light of Integration.

The Light of Integration, not only of the seven rays but also of the so-called secret rays, the higher spiritual rays that shall now be anchored through the light that this messenger feels, as I am speaking these words in this public location, unbeknownst to those who are going by on their curiosity tours and unbeknownst to those who will be going by here in their work as

Senators and Congressmen and members of the American government who have, of course, very little awareness of the Buddha or very little allegiance to the Buddha.

Nevertheless, is not one of the principles of this nation precisely that out of the many, out of the diversity, is formed a union? A greater union that is allegiance to higher principles and to the absolute God victory of the completing of the circle. Whereby you first have the one indivisible God that divides itself into many self-aware extensions of itself; and then, through the process of the growth in self-awareness, those self-aware extensions come together, transcend their differences without losing their individuality, and then form a greater union here below that is a reflection of the greater union that exists Above.

This is indeed the purpose of this nation, as it is the purpose of any nation and of the family of nations throughout the world: that matter becomes a reflection of Spirit through the free-will choices of each human being, aligning itself with its presence, with its I AM Presence, with its I Will Be Presence. Then, through that union with the Spirit that is vertical, it sees also beyond the outer differences and therefore can come into a horizontal union that is beyond anything that could be achieved through the outer mind, through the separate self, through the ego.

"One nation under God" means precisely that this nation is built on the recognition that there are higher principles that must transcend anything that comes up, and/or is defined here below. It is truly a reflection of the fact that there are higher principles that transcend anything that can be brought forth and defined through the fallen consciousness, the consciousness of separation, the consciousness of duality that is always focused on dualistic polarities.

13 | The need to transcend representative democracy

An outdated governmental model

You do indeed see this consciousness reflected here in this United States Capitol building and in the fact that this nation, supposed to be one nation under God, still has this outdated model of having two chambers that need to debate endlessly, sometimes, and often cannot come to a resolution because they cannot see beyond the outer differences. Thus, would it not be possible, then, to have a new approach, a higher approach, whereby we seek to find a new approach to union, a new approach to coming together and finding a way to go beyond the differences?

That way would, of course, be to just have one legislative chamber but also to make sure that this chamber does not have as much power as is currently enjoyed by the Senate and the Congress. For they are simply administrators who administer the will of the people, and it is the will of the people that is allowed to make the major decisions and the major laws through a direct vote by the people. There are indeed many in the United States who are hung up on the idea that the United States is a republic that does not necessarily reflect the will of the majority, but is based on certain principles that the majority cannot overrule, and that Congress, the Senate, the President and the Supreme Court supposedly cannot overrule either.

Nevertheless, it is necessary to take this democracy to the next logical step in its evolution. It is necessary to recognize that with modern communication and information technology, there is no longer the need for the kind of representative democracy that this nation has had so far. There is a need for a more direct involvement of the people. Indeed, if the people will disregard or overrule certain eternal principles, then they must be allowed to do so and feel and experience the consequences of their choices. In the end, how are the people to learn? Again, of course, the absolute purpose for this nation is not to produce a certain outer result; it is to further the growth in awareness of the people. That is why this nation is *of* the people, *by* the people and *for* the growth in consciousness of the people.

They will grow only by governing themselves and seeing the consequences so that they decide to educate themselves and make better choices in the future than they have made in the past. This is the one and only way that growth can happen. It is the only way that this nation can fulfill its destiny. It is the only way that this nation can grow beyond the current state where, too often, a single word is used to characterize the current state of American government and that word is, as you know: gridlock.

Transcending representative democracy

Gridlock—because there is not the willingness to look beyond conditions on earth, conditions in the matter realm, and decide that we are spiritual beings who will not adapt to conditions in matter. We will take command over conditions in matter, and we will co-create the conditions that we want to see, instead of feeling like we are victims of forces beyond our control.

This is the lesson for all people who take embodiment on earth, and it is, of course, only a logical consequence of this that democracy was founded. Where you do not have a dictator, you do not even have a divinely ordained ruler who tells you what is the will of God. You must tune in individually to what is the higher will for your own life, and for the life of the nation, and for the life of humanity. There is no longer validity in a representative democracy. There is no longer validity in a vicarious atonement where other people do something for you or for the population.

We cannot anymore support and sponsor any form of government that is based on any philosophy that does not acknowledge the right and the need of the people to govern themselves. This is not sustainable in the Aquarian age. It will not be sustainable, and you will see that countries who are not willing to move higher will experience one crisis after another. You have seen recently in Egypt what happened when a dictator was not willing to step back. You will see this indeed roll around the planet in coming years. There is not a nation that will not be tested on its willingness to transcend its current state, whatever that may be.

You may look at America and compare it to Egypt and say, Egypt had a dictator for 30 years and United States has had a democracy for 200 years or more. Nevertheless, I tell you, it is not only a matter of what state a country has been in. What matters in the Aquarian age is the country's willingness to transcend its current state no matter what that state is. We are not here seeking a particular outer goal where all nations in the world have the same form of government. We are seeking continued growth in the consciousness of the people. Continued growth can happen in only one way: by transcending the state you are in right now.

There is no other way to grow, for the moment you stop transcending, you will stagnate. You will stop where you are. You will not be able to go beyond your current state until you again are willing to question the unquestionable, to rethink, to tune in to your higher self and get a different perspective.

This, then, is the Flame that I anchor here in even greater intensity than before. You will see, if you can see with the inner eye, a Golden Buddha figure right here in the center of this Rotunda, and the head of it is about the height of the dome.

This is the magnitude of the Flame that I anchor here to hold that balance for the American nation, as it will face severe testings in the coming years. Thus, this is my commitment to forging a greater alliance between East and West so that we may have that horizontal oneness forming the foundation for the vertical oneness. As Above, so below. Thus, I have completed the anchoring of this Flame, and thus my release is complete.

Therefore I seal the release of this Living Word in the Flame that I AM. Gautama, I AM!

14 | INVOKING DIRECT DEMOCRACY

In the name of the I AM THAT I AM, Jesus Christ, I use the authority that I have as a being in embodiment on earth to call upon Gautama Buddha to reinforce my calls and use my chakras to project the statements in this invocation into the collective consciousness and awaken Americans to the need to go beyond representative democracy to a more direct form of democracy. Awaken Americans to the reality that we are spiritual beings and that we can co-create a new future by working with the ascended masters. I especially call for ...

[Make your own calls here.]

Part 1

1. I invoke the Presence of Gautama Buddha, anchored in the Rotunda of the United States Capitol, manifest as the Light of Integration.

Gautama, show my mental state
that does give rise to love and hate,
your exposé I do endure,
so my perception will be pure.

**Gautama, Flame of Cosmic Peace,
unruly thoughts do hereby cease,
we radiate from you and me
the peace to still Samsara's Sea.**

2. I invoke the Light of Integration, not only of the Seven Rays but also of the Secret Rays, the higher spiritual rays. I call for it to inspire those who go by here in their work as Senators and Congressmen and members of the American government.

Gautama, in your Flame of Peace,
the struggling self I now release,
the Buddha Nature I now see,
it is the core of you and me.

**Gautama, Flame of Cosmic Peace,
unruly thoughts do hereby cease,
we radiate from you and me
the peace to still Samsara's Sea.**

3. I invoke the awakening of the thoughtful people of America to the realization that one of the principles of this nation is that out of the many, out of the diversity, is formed a Union.

Gautama, I am one with thee,
Mara's demons do now flee,
your Presence like a soothing balm,
my mind and senses ever calm.

**Gautama, Flame of Cosmic Peace,
unruly thoughts do hereby cease,
we radiate from you and me
the peace to still Samsara's Sea.**

4. I invoke the awakening of the thoughtful people of America to the realization that America is meant to be a Greater Union that has allegiance to higher principles and to the absolute God Victory of the completing of the circle.

Gautama, I now take the vow,
to live in the eternal now,
with you I do transcend all time,
to live in present so sublime.

**Gautama, Flame of Cosmic Peace,
unruly thoughts do hereby cease,
we radiate from you and me
the peace to still Samsara's Sea.**

5. I invoke the awakening of the thoughtful people of America to the realization that the first principle is the one Indivisible God that divides itself into many self-aware extensions of itself.

Gautama, I have no desire,
to nothing earthly I aspire,
in non-attachment I now rest,
passing Mara's subtle test.

**Gautama, Flame of Cosmic Peace,
unruly thoughts do hereby cease,
we radiate from you and me
the peace to still Samsara's Sea.**

6. I invoke the awakening of the thoughtful people of America to the realization that through the process of the growth in self-awareness, those self-aware extensions come together, transcend their differences without losing their individuality, and then form a greater union here below that is a reflection of the Greater Union that exists Above.

> Gautama, I melt into you,
> my mind is one, no longer two,
> immersed in your resplendent glow,
> Nirvana is all that I know.

**Gautama, Flame of Cosmic Peace,
unruly thoughts do hereby cease,
we radiate from you and me
the peace to still Samsara's Sea.**

7. I invoke the awakening of the thoughtful people of America to the realization that the purpose of this nation is that matter becomes a reflection of Spirit through the free-will choices of each human being, aligning itself with its Presence.

> Gautama, in your timeless space,
> I am immersed in Cosmic Grace,
> I know the God beyond all form,
> to world I will no more conform.

14 | Invoking direct democracy

> **Gautama, Flame of Cosmic Peace,**
> **unruly thoughts do hereby cease,**
> **we radiate from you and me**
> **the peace to still Samsara's Sea.**

8. I invoke the awakening of the thoughtful people of America to the realization that through the union with the Spirit that is vertical, we see beyond the outer differences and therefore can come into a horizontal union that is beyond anything that could be achieved through the outer mind, through the separate self, through the ego.

> Gautama, I am now awake,
> I clearly see what is at stake,
> and thus I claim my sacred right
> to be on earth the Buddhic Light.

> **Gautama, Flame of Cosmic Peace,**
> **unruly thoughts do hereby cease,**
> **we radiate from you and me**
> **the peace to still Samsara's Sea.**

9. I invoke the awakening of the thoughtful people of America to the realization that "One Nation under God" means that this nation is built on the recognition that there are higher principles that must transcend anything defined here below.

> Gautama, with your thunderbolt,
> we give the earth a mighty jolt,
> I know that some will understand,
> and join the Buddha's timeless band.

> Gautama, Flame of Cosmic Peace,
> unruly thoughts do hereby cease,
> we radiate from you and me
> the peace to still Samsara's Sea.

Part 2

1. I invoke the awakening of the thoughtful people of America to the realization that there are higher principles that transcend anything that can be brought forth and defined through the fallen consciousness, the consciousness of separation, the consciousness of duality, that is always focused on dualistic polarities.

> Gautama, show my mental state
> that does give rise to love and hate,
> your exposé I do endure,
> so my perception will be pure.

> **Gautama, Flame of Cosmic Peace,**
> **unruly thoughts do hereby cease,**
> **we radiate from you and me**
> **the peace to still Samsara's Sea.**

2. I invoke the awakening of the thoughtful people of America to the realization that although this nation is supposed to be One Nation under God, it still has this outdated model of having two chambers that need to debate endlessly and often cannot come to a resolution because they cannot see beyond the outer differences.

> Gautama, in your Flame of Peace,
> the struggling self I now release,
> the Buddha Nature I now see,
> it is the core of you and me.
>
> **Gautama, Flame of Cosmic Peace,**
> **unruly thoughts do hereby cease,**
> **we radiate from you and me**
> **the peace to still Samsara's Sea.**

3. I invoke the awakening of the thoughtful people of America to the realization that it is possible to have a new approach, a higher approach, whereby we seek to find a new approach to union, a new approach to coming together and finding a way to go beyond the differences.

> Gautama, I am one with thee,
> Mara's demons do now flee,
> your Presence like a soothing balm,
> my mind and senses ever calm.
>
> **Gautama, Flame of Cosmic Peace,**
> **unruly thoughts do hereby cease,**
> **we radiate from you and me**
> **the peace to still Samsara's Sea.**

4. I invoke the awakening of the thoughtful people of America to the realization that we need to have just one legislative chamber, but we also need to make sure that this chamber does not have as much power as is currently enjoyed by the Senate and the Congress.

Gautama, I now take the vow,
to live in the eternal now,
with you I do transcend all time,
to live in present so sublime.

**Gautama, Flame of Cosmic Peace,
unruly thoughts do hereby cease,
we radiate from you and me
the peace to still Samsara's Sea.**

5. I invoke the awakening of the thoughtful people of America to the realization that the representatives are simply administrators who administer the will of the people.

Gautama, I have no desire,
to nothing earthly I aspire,
in non-attachment I now rest,
passing Mara's subtle test.

**Gautama, Flame of Cosmic Peace,
unruly thoughts do hereby cease,
we radiate from you and me
the peace to still Samsara's Sea.**

6. I invoke the awakening of the thoughtful people of America to the realization that it is the will of the people that should be allowed to make the major decisions and the major laws through a direct vote by the people.

Gautama, I melt into you,
my mind is one, no longer two,
immersed in your resplendent glow,
Nirvana is all that I know.

**Gautama, Flame of Cosmic Peace,
unruly thoughts do hereby cease,
we radiate from you and me
the peace to still Samsara's Sea.**

7. I invoke the awakening of the thoughtful people of America to the realization that many Americans are hung up on the idea that the United States is a Republic.

Gautama, in your timeless space,
I am immersed in Cosmic Grace,
I know the God beyond all form,
to world I will no more conform.

**Gautama, Flame of Cosmic Peace,
unruly thoughts do hereby cease,
we radiate from you and me
the peace to still Samsara's Sea.**

8. I invoke the awakening of the thoughtful people of America to the realization that some say a republic does not necessarily reflect the will of the majority, but is based on certain principles that the majority cannot overrule and that Congress, the Senate, the President and the Supreme Court supposedly cannot overrule either.

Gautama, I am now awake,
I clearly see what is at stake,
and thus I claim my sacred right
to be on earth the Buddhic Light.

> Gautama, Flame of Cosmic Peace,
> unruly thoughts do hereby cease,
> we radiate from you and me
> the peace to still Samsara's Sea.

9. I invoke the awakening of the thoughtful people of America to the realization that it is necessary to take this democracy to the next logical step in its evolution.

> Gautama, with your thunderbolt,
> we give the earth a mighty jolt,
> I know that some will understand,
> and join the Buddha's timeless band.

> **Gautama, Flame of Cosmic Peace,
> unruly thoughts do hereby cease,
> we radiate from you and me
> the peace to still Samsara's Sea.**

Part 3

1. I invoke the awakening of the thoughtful people of America to the realization that with modern communication and information technology, there is no longer the need for the kind of representative democracy that this nation has had so far.

> Gautama, show my mental state
> that does give rise to love and hate,
> your exposé I do endure,
> so my perception will be pure.

14 | Invoking direct democracy

> **Gautama, Flame of Cosmic Peace,**
> **unruly thoughts do hereby cease,**
> **we radiate from you and me**
> **the peace to still Samsara's Sea.**

2. I invoke the awakening of the thoughtful people of America to the realization that there is a need for a more direct involvement of the people.

> Gautama, in your Flame of Peace,
> the struggling self I now release,
> the Buddha Nature I now see,
> it is the core of you and me.

> **Gautama, Flame of Cosmic Peace,**
> **unruly thoughts do hereby cease,**
> **we radiate from you and me**
> **the peace to still Samsara's Sea.**

3. I invoke the awakening of the thoughtful people of America to the realization that if the people will disregard or overrule certain eternal principles, then they must be allowed to do so and feel and experience the consequences of their choices. For in the end, how are the people to learn?

> Gautama, I am one with thee,
> Mara's demons do now flee,
> your Presence like a soothing balm,
> my mind and senses ever calm.

> **Gautama, Flame of Cosmic Peace,**
> **unruly thoughts do hereby cease,**
> **we radiate from you and me**
> **the peace to still Samsara's Sea.**

4. I invoke the awakening of the thoughtful people of America to the realization that the absolute purpose for this nation is not to produce a certain outer result; it is to further the growth in awareness of the people. That is why this nation is *of* the people, *by* the people and *for* the growth in consciousness of the people.

> Gautama, I now take the vow,
> to live in the eternal now,
> with you I do transcend all time,
> to live in present so sublime.

> **Gautama, Flame of Cosmic Peace,**
> **unruly thoughts do hereby cease,**
> **we radiate from you and me**
> **the peace to still Samsara's Sea.**

5. I invoke the awakening of the thoughtful people of America to the realization that people will grow only by governing themselves and seeing the consequences so that they decide to educate themselves and make better choices in the future than they have made in the past.

> Gautama, I have no desire,
> to nothing earthly I aspire,
> in non-attachment I now rest,
> passing Mara's subtle test.

**Gautama, Flame of Cosmic Peace,
unruly thoughts do hereby cease,
we radiate from you and me
the peace to still Samsara's Sea.**

6. I invoke the awakening of the thoughtful people of America to the realization that this is the one and only way that growth can happen. It is the only way that this nation can fulfill its destiny.

Gautama, I melt into you,
my mind is one, no longer two,
immersed in your resplendent glow,
Nirvana is all that I know.

**Gautama, Flame of Cosmic Peace,
unruly thoughts do hereby cease,
we radiate from you and me
the peace to still Samsara's Sea.**

7. I invoke the awakening of the thoughtful people of America to the realization that this is the only way that this nation can grow beyond the current state where the American government is often bogged down by gridlock.

Gautama, in your timeless space,
I am immersed in Cosmic Grace,
I know the God beyond all form,
to world I will no more conform.

> **Gautama, Flame of Cosmic Peace,**
> **unruly thoughts do hereby cease,**
> **we radiate from you and me**
> **the peace to still Samsara's Sea.**

8. I invoke the awakening of the thoughtful people of America to the realization that there is gridlock because there is not the willingness to look beyond conditions on earth, conditions in the matter realm, and decide that we are spiritual beings who will not adapt to conditions in matter.

> Gautama, I am now awake,
> I clearly see what is at stake,
> and thus I claim my sacred right
> to be on earth the Buddhic Light.

> **Gautama, Flame of Cosmic Peace,**
> **unruly thoughts do hereby cease,**
> **we radiate from you and me**
> **the peace to still Samsara's Sea.**

9. I invoke the awakening of the thoughtful people of America to the realization that we need to take command over conditions in matter and co-create the conditions that we want to see, instead of feeling like we are victims of forces beyond our control.

> Gautama, with your thunderbolt,
> we give the earth a mighty jolt,
> I know that some will understand,
> and join the Buddha's timeless band.

**Gautama, Flame of Cosmic Peace,
unruly thoughts do hereby cease,
we radiate from you and me
the peace to still Samsara's Sea.**

Part 4

1. I invoke the awakening of the thoughtful people of America to the realization that this is the lesson for all people who take embodiment on earth, and it is a logical consequence of this that democracy was founded.

Gautama, show my mental state
that does give rise to love and hate,
your exposé I do endure,
so my perception will be pure.

**Gautama, Flame of Cosmic Peace,
unruly thoughts do hereby cease,
we radiate from you and me
the peace to still Samsara's Sea.**

2. I invoke the awakening of the thoughtful people of America to the realization that we need to experience that we do not have a dictator, we do not even have a divinely ordained ruler who tells us what is the will of God.

Gautama, in your Flame of Peace,
the struggling self I now release,
the Buddha Nature I now see,
it is the core of you and me.

> **Gautama, Flame of Cosmic Peace,**
> **unruly thoughts do hereby cease,**
> **we radiate from you and me**
> **the peace to still Samsara's Sea.**

3. I invoke the awakening of the thoughtful people of America to the realization that we must tune in individually to what is the higher will for our own lives, for the nation and for humanity.

> Gautama, I am one with thee,
> Mara's demons do now flee,
> your Presence like a soothing balm,
> my mind and senses ever calm.

> **Gautama, Flame of Cosmic Peace,**
> **unruly thoughts do hereby cease,**
> **we radiate from you and me**
> **the peace to still Samsara's Sea.**

4. I invoke the awakening of the thoughtful people of America to the realization that there is no longer validity in a representative democracy. There is no longer validity in a vicarious atonement where other people do something for us or for the population.

> Gautama, I now take the vow,
> to live in the eternal now,
> with you I do transcend all time,
> to live in present so sublime.

> **Gautama, Flame of Cosmic Peace,**
> **unruly thoughts do hereby cease,**
> **we radiate from you and me**
> **the peace to still Samsara's Sea.**

5. I invoke the awakening of the thoughtful people of America to the realization that the ascended masters cannot anymore support and sponsor a government that is based on any philosophy that does not acknowledge the right and the need of the people to govern themselves. This is not sustainable in the Aquarian age.

> Gautama, I have no desire,
> to nothing earthly I aspire,
> in non-attachment I now rest,
> passing Mara's subtle test.

> **Gautama, Flame of Cosmic Peace,**
> **unruly thoughts do hereby cease,**
> **we radiate from you and me**
> **the peace to still Samsara's Sea.**

6. I invoke the awakening of the thoughtful people of America to the realization that what matters in the Aquarian Age is the country's willingness to transcend its current state, no matter what that state is.

> Gautama, I melt into you,
> my mind is one, no longer two,
> immersed in your resplendent glow,
> Nirvana is all that I know.

> Gautama, Flame of Cosmic Peace,
> unruly thoughts do hereby cease,
> we radiate from you and me
> the peace to still Samsara's Sea.

7. I invoke the awakening of the thoughtful people of America to the realization that continued growth can happen in only one way: by transcending the state we are in right now. The moment we stop transcending, we will stagnate. We will not be able to go beyond our current state until we again are willing to question the unquestionable.

> Gautama, in your timeless space,
> I am immersed in Cosmic Grace,
> I know the God beyond all form,
> to world I will no more conform.

> Gautama, Flame of Cosmic Peace,
> unruly thoughts do hereby cease,
> we radiate from you and me
> the peace to still Samsara's Sea.

8. I invoke the Flame that Gautama has anchored, and I see a Golden Buddha figure right in the center of the Rotunda, filling the entire space.

> Gautama, I am now awake,
> I clearly see what is at stake,
> and thus I claim my sacred right
> to be on earth the Buddhic Light.

**Gautama, Flame of Cosmic Peace,
unruly thoughts do hereby cease,
we radiate from you and me
the peace to still Samsara's Sea.**

9. I call for the Flame of Gautama Buddha to hold the balance for the American nation and forge a greater alliance between East and West, so that we may have that horizontal oneness forming the foundation for the vertical oneness of as Above, so below.

Gautama, with your thunderbolt,
we give the earth a mighty jolt,
I know that some will understand,
and join the Buddha's timeless band.

**Gautama, Flame of Cosmic Peace,
unruly thoughts do hereby cease,
we radiate from you and me
the peace to still Samsara's Sea.**

Sealing

In the name of the I AM THAT I AM, I accept that Archangel Michael, Astrea and Shiva form an impenetrable shield around myself and all constructive people, sealing us from all fear-based energies in all four octaves. I accept that the Light of God is consuming and transforming all fear-based energies that make up the dark forces working against America!

15 | THE TRUE ALCHEMY OF FREEDOM

This dictation was given in an open area East of the Capitol and between the Supreme Court building and the Library of Congress building in Washington, D.C.

Saint Germain with Portia I AM, and I AM here! I am here to anchor the Flame of the Seventh Ray, right here between these two buildings of the Supreme Court of the United States and the Library of Congress. Why does the Goddess of Justice carry the scales? Because there are two sides to justice: You cannot have justice without freedom. You cannot have justice without having the freedom of knowing what you need to know in order to meter out justice. Thus, you see on one side the Supreme Court building, with the Supreme Court judges. But how can they sit in this Greco-Roman temple – that they have erected to keep them boxed up – and meter out justice without having full knowledge of what is going on in the nation or in the material universe? Thus, they need what is next door, the knowledge that is stored.

Of course, when you see the symbol for justice – the scales – you see that there are two bowls. But are they not hanging from a central point, the top of the triangle, the top of the pyramid? So is it enough to meter out justice to have the horizontal knowledge stored in this Library of Congress, the knowledge of this world? Nay, of course, it is not enough! For there must be the singularity, the open door, so that a higher knowledge, a higher vision, a higher matrix can descend. It should indeed – under ideal circumstances – descend upon both the Congress and the Senate – or rather the one legislative chamber that is all that is needed – and the Supreme Court and, of course, also upon the President.

Self-government requires knowledge of self

Yet if we indeed could get the Supreme Court judges and the Senators and Congressmen to be open to a higher knowledge, then we would have made considerable progress towards this higher union that is "*of* the people, *by* the people, *for* the people" but truly is "*of* God, *by* God and *for* God." For can there be self-government unless there is an acknowledgment of what the Self is?

What is the Self that is capable of governing? It is not the separate self; this I trust you can see. Thus, as Hilarion so eloquently explained, no one below the 48th level of consciousness should be involved with the government of a free, truly democratic nation. How can you be free when you are identified with the separate self that can never fathom freedom, but only wants to restrict freedom based on its own vision, the vision it has created by taking upon itself the power to be a god who defines good and evil. This can never lead to Freedom, but only to one form of tyranny after another. Thus, you saw the Founding Fathers who were, most of them, above and well above the 48th level of consciousness. You saw them be able to receive a higher vision of the Declaration of Independence and the Constitution of this nation, and they attempted to embody it. But when faced with the actual reality of administering things in the physical octave – dealing with the laws that have been created through humankind's collective consciousness – well, then they found it very difficult to implement their vision, as the initial chaos of this nation clearly demonstrates. As you see demonstrated throughout the history of this nation where no sooner had a nation been established based on rights than those rights started to be undermined by elite groups who saw no reason to give the people rights. For they wanted the people to remain as the slaves of the elite.

International bankers undermining democracy

Thus, they have attempted to enslave them by undermining the democratic institutions and democratic freedoms. They have especially attempted to do this through the money system. Do you not recognize that there were international bankers who financed the British in the Revolutionary War, and even in secret ways, found ways to finance the revolutionary forces? George Washington was one of the few who acknowledged this and attempted to keep himself and the nation independent of it.

Not long after his presidency was over, indeed some of these international bankers managed to write themselves into American government and American life through an unholy bank charter that should never have been given to anyone and was from the start unconstitutional, against the spirit of the revolution and the constitution. So, you see how even up to very recent times, these bankers have managed to deceive the government into letting the people once again guarantee the loans from the elite with their life-blood, with their labor that is all they have to give.

What is, then, to prevent a collapse of the financial system of this nation when the people are faced with the inevitable situation of either no employment or higher prices on necessities? Was it not indeed the higher prices on daily necessities that sparked the uprisings in Tunisia and Egypt? Is it not indeed foreseeable by anyone with common sense that this will spread beyond these two nations? For there are many other nations where the people are living under such poor circumstances that they can barely feed their families.

Virtual slavery through mortgages

Is it really necessary that the economy of the United States needs to become so bad that people can no longer feed their families, in order for the people to realize that they need to educate themselves about the economy and the financial system? So that they can see how money is being used to create a slavery that might not appear as slavery, but it truly binds the people as much as the feudal societies where no peasant was allowed to move away from the land of the landlord to which he belonged. Is it not so that the American people cannot in many cases move away from their homes that belong to the mortgage companies, for they have no way of selling the homes for a price anywhere near what they owe on them.

Well, is it, then, not necessary to consider: "To whom do we owe this money?" Who owns the debt? Where does the debt come from? Who is collecting the interest off the debt? You see, the debt is backed by the government but does the government collect the interest? Nay, the private banks of the power elite collect the interest. Can you not see, then, that there is a need to revolutionize the entire system and say that when real estate prices were artificially raised and now have collapsed, then it is no longer right that the people should owe an artificial debt. The debt on a house should be reflected by the market value of that property and not some previous artificially created bubble value that has nothing to do with anything real.

The fear of a free economy

This, then, is just one revolutionary thought that will come from this Flame of Freedom that I am anchoring here in this place. Again, as with the other flames we have anchored, the effect of this flame will be to challenge the assumptions, the mental boxes, that have created the current situation. Where there is not only gridlock in this Capitol building, but there is gridlock in the Supreme Court, there is gridlock in the financial system, there is gridlock in the economy. Because the power elite, in their fear of a free economy, have attempted to clamp down on the financial system so that money cannot flow freely. When it cannot flow freely, how can it then be multiplied and how can the economy grow?

You cannot force an economy to grow, and indeed the power elite know this. They do not want to force the economy to grow, for they fear economic growth. They know that they cannot control it when the economy is growing beyond a certain level. Therefore, they seek to maintain economic growth below a certain level—and when they cannot, they panic and then they precipitate a crisis that then crashes the economy. Then, they feel, they again have some control. This is the cycle of inflated growth and then inflated non-growth, inflated collapse, that you have seen in the American economy almost from the beginning—and that you will only see accelerate, unless the people stand up to it and say: "No more! We will not accept that the money system in these United States is not controlled by Congress, who are elected and who are constitutionally authorized to do so. We will no longer tolerate this, and therefore we do not want the Federal Reserve to be in control of the money system. We demand that Congress takes back its constitutional power as the only authority that has the right to print money."

Unless this happens, then there must be chaos and turmoil until the people are willing to rethink, to reeducate themselves, to let their old sense that "all is well with the American Dream" die. So that America might be reborn when the people's vision of America is reborn and is no longer trapped in these old mental boxes created by the power elite.

The descent of the Freedom Flame

Let this Freedom Flame descend, and let it take command of the American Nation. So that those who are the enemies of freedom can no longer hide, and will be challenged to choose life or to choose death—for there is nothing in between. If you are not free, you are enslaved. You may not think you are enslaved because you have fooled yourself – based on some illusion or other – to think that you still live in a free nation. You have fooled yourself into being able to overlook this, that or the next encroachment upon your freedom so that you still maintain a sense of equilibrium that as long as this or that has not happened, we are still a free nation.

15 | The true alchemy of freedom

Wake up NOW, all Americans, I say! Recognize the fact that you are no longer a free nation and that you have not been a free nation for a very long time. In fact, you have never lived up to the highest ideal and potential for a truly free nation. Now, wake up and claim true freedom. Reach for that vision of true freedom. Claim it, and then be willing to demand that your government embodies it.

Take a stand for life! For right now you are not even taking a stand for death. You are sitting down, you are sleeping on your watch. You have been lulled asleep by the good life, but do you not see that the good life is crumbling around you? So take heed, then, and wake up before the chaos can no longer be turned back. One way or another, change will come. One way or another, this nation will achieve greater freedom economically and in any other way. For there is no other way to bring the Golden Age than to break down the prison walls that are holding back change.

The inevitability of change

Change will come. The Flame of Freedom makes change inevitable. There is no way to stop this, there is no power on earth – neither the power elite, nor even the will of the majority of the people – that can stop this. For there are enough people in embodiment who have gone close to or beyond the 96th level of consciousness who have demanded greater freedom. Then, when they come together in sufficient numbers, they can actually outweigh the will of the majority. This is how you have true self-government where the majority is pulled up by the creative elite, by the top 10%, and more than the top 10%, who are willing to reach for a higher vision. Thus, even if the majority are not willing to reach for that vision, they cannot hold back the change, the floodgates of change.

As you have even seen in Egypt where it was truly not a majority of the people that backed the revolution. For most of them still wanted to stay asleep with what they had. But there was a critical mass of people who grasped that higher vision, and who were willing to take a stand for it and to keep standing even when many among their family members said that it was ridiculous and it was time to go home. But they kept standing until the dictator had to stand down.

Thus, the same needs to happen in this nation where the power elite – and even the government apparatus that is out of touch with freedom – must be forced to see the handwriting on the wall. They have to make concessions, they have to change the system they have created, they have to step down from their self-created pedestals, as you indeed see in these buildings that are elevated above the people.

How can you have a capitol city of a free democratic nation, where the government is supposed to be *of* the people, *by* the people, *for* the people, and yet each single building that houses the government is raised up on a pedestal and therefore indeed above the people? Do you not see, even the symbolism of this architecture is out of touch with the Flame of Freedom that I AM!

I AM the Flame of Freedom! I AM Saint Germain and I AM here to see this change through to the golden age vision that I AM! I do not hold a vision as an external vision; I embody it as the true alchemist. I have become the Golden Age! I AM the Golden Age! Lock in to my Presence that you may be the Golden Age here below as I AM the Golden Age Above. As Above, so below. You and I: One. Out of the One: Many. Out of the Many: One. This is alchemy, and I AM here!

16 | INVOKING THE TRUE ALCHEMY OF FREEDOM

In the name of the I AM THAT I AM, Jesus Christ, I use the authority that I have as a being in embodiment on earth to call upon Saint Germain to reinforce my calls and use my chakras to project the statements in this invocation into the collective consciousness and awaken Americans to the spiritual meaning of freedom. Awaken Americans to the reality that we are spiritual beings and that we can co-create a new future by working with the ascended masters. I especially call for …

[Make your own calls here.]

Part 1

1. I invoke the Flame of the Seventh Ray that Saint Germain has anchored between the Supreme Court of the United States and the Library of Congress.

O Saint Germain, you do inspire,
my vision raised forever higher,
with you I form a figure-eight,
your Golden Age I co-create.

O Saint Germain, what love you bring,
it truly makes all matter sing,
your violet flame does all restore,
with you we are becoming more.

2. I invoke the awakening of the freedom-loving people of America to the realization that the Goddess of Justice carries the scales because there are two sides to justice: We cannot have justice without freedom.

O Saint Germain, what Freedom Flame,
released when we recite your name,
acceleration is your gift,
our planet it will surely lift.

O Saint Germain, what love you bring,
it truly makes all matter sing,
your violet flame does all restore,
with you we are becoming more.

3. I invoke the awakening of the freedom-loving people of America to the realization that we cannot have justice without having the freedom of knowing what we need to know in order to meter out justice.

16 | Invoking the true alchemy of freedom

> O Saint Germain, in love we claim,
> our right to bring your violet flame,
> from you Above, to us below,
> it is an all-transforming flow.
>
> **O Saint Germain, what love you bring,**
> **it truly makes all matter sing,**
> **your violet flame does all restore,**
> **with you we are becoming more.**

4. I invoke the awakening of the freedom-loving people of America to the realization that the Supreme Court judges cannot meter out justice without having full knowledge of what is going on in the nation or in the material universe.

> O Saint Germain, I love you so,
> my aura filled with violet glow,
> my chakras filled with violet fire,
> I am your cosmic amplifier.
>
> **O Saint Germain, what love you bring,**
> **it truly makes all matter sing,**
> **your violet flame does all restore,**
> **with you we are becoming more.**

5. I invoke the awakening of the freedom-loving people of America to the realization that the symbol for justice is the scales, which has two bowls that are hanging from a central point, the top of the triangle, the top of the pyramid.

O Saint Germain, I am now free,
your violet flame is therapy,
transform all hang-ups in my mind,
as inner peace I surely find.

**O Saint Germain, what love you bring,
it truly makes all matter sing,
your violet flame does all restore,
with you we are becoming more.**

6. I invoke the awakening of the freedom-loving people of America to the realization that in order to meter out justice, it is not enough to have the horizontal knowledge stored in the Library of Congress, the knowledge of this world.

O Saint Germain, my body pure,
your violet flame for all is cure,
consume the cause of all disease,
and therefore I am all at ease.

**O Saint Germain, what love you bring,
it truly makes all matter sing,
your violet flame does all restore,
with you we are becoming more.**

7. I invoke the awakening of the freedom-loving people of America to the realization that justice must be based on the singularity, the open door, so that a higher knowledge, a higher vision, a higher matrix can descend.

O Saint Germain, I'm karma-free,
the past no longer burdens me,
a brand new opportunity,
I am in Christic unity.

**O Saint Germain, what love you bring,
it truly makes all matter sing,
your violet flame does all restore,
with you we are becoming more.**

8. I call forth this higher knowledge to descend upon the Congress and the Senate – or rather the one legislative chamber that is all that is needed – the Supreme Court and the President.

O Saint Germain, we are now one,
I am for you a violet sun,
as we transform this planet earth,
your Golden Age is given birth.

**O Saint Germain, what love you bring,
it truly makes all matter sing,
your violet flame does all restore,
with you we are becoming more.**

9. I invoke the awakening of the freedom-loving people of America to the realization that if we could get the Supreme Court judges, the Senators and Congressmen to be open to a higher knowledge, we would have made progress towards a higher union.

> O Saint Germain, the earth is free,
> from burden of duality,
> in oneness we bring what is best,
> your Golden Age is manifest.
>
> **O Saint Germain, what love you bring,**
> **it truly makes all matter sing,**
> **your violet flame does all restore,**
> **with you we are becoming more.**

Part 2

1. I invoke the awakening of the freedom-loving people of America to the realization that a higher union must be "of the people, by the people, for the people" but truly is "of God, by God and for God." For can there be self-government unless there is an acknowledgment of what the Self is?

> O Portia, in your own retreat,
> with Mother's Love you do me greet.
> As all my tests I now complete,
> old patterns I no more repeat.
>
> **O Portia, opportunity,**
> **I am beyond duality.**
> **I focus now internally,**
> **with you I grow eternally.**

2. I invoke the awakening of the freedom-loving people of America to the realization that the Self that is capable of governing is not the separate self.

16 | Invoking the true alchemy of freedom

> O Portia, Justice is your name,
> upholding Cosmic Honor Flame,
> No longer will I play the game,
> of seeking to remain the same.
>
> **O Portia, opportunity,**
> **I am beyond duality.**
> **I focus now internally,**
> **with you I grow eternally.**

3. I invoke the awakening of the freedom-loving people of America to the realization that no one below the 48th level of consciousness should be involved with the government of a free, truly democratic nation.

> O Portia, in the cosmic flow,
> one with you, I ever grow.
> I am the chalice here below,
> of cosmic justice you bestow.
>
> **O Portia, opportunity,**
> **I am beyond duality.**
> **I focus now internally,**
> **with you I grow eternally.**

4. I invoke the awakening of the freedom-loving people of America to the realization that we cannot be free when we are identified with the separate self.

> O Portia, cosmic balance bring,
> eternal hope, my heart does sing.
> Protected by your Mother's wing,
> I feel at one with everything.

**O Portia, opportunity,
I am beyond duality.
I focus now internally,
with you I grow eternally.**

5. I invoke the awakening of the freedom-loving people of America to the realization that the separate self can never fathom freedom. It only wants to restrict freedom based on its own vision, the vision it has created by taking upon itself the power to be a god who defines good and evil.

O Portia, bring the Mother Light,
to set all free from darkest night.
Your Love Flame shines forever bright,
with Saint Germain now hold me tight.

**O Portia, opportunity,
I am beyond duality.
I focus now internally,
with you I grow eternally.**

6. I invoke the awakening of the freedom-loving people of America to the realization that this can never lead to freedom, but only to one form of tyranny after another.

O Portia, in your mastery,
I feel transforming chemistry.
In your light of reality,
I find the golden alchemy.

16 | Invoking the true alchemy of freedom

**O Portia, opportunity,
I am beyond duality.
I focus now internally,
with you I grow eternally.**

7. I invoke the awakening of the freedom-loving people of America to the realization that the Founding Fathers were above the 48th level of consciousness, and thus able to receive a higher vision of the Declaration of Independence and the Constitution of this nation.

O Portia, in the cosmic stream,
I am awake from human dream.
Removing now the ego's beam,
I earn my place on cosmic team.

**O Portia, opportunity,
I am beyond duality.
I focus now internally,
with you I grow eternally.**

8. I invoke the awakening of the freedom-loving people of America to the realization that when faced with the actual reality of administering things in the physical octave, the Founding Fathers found it very difficult to implement their vision.

O Portia, you come from afar,
you are a cosmic avatar.
So infinite your repertoire,
you are for earth a guiding star.

**O Portia, opportunity,
I am beyond duality.
I focus now internally,
with you I grow eternally.**

9. I invoke the awakening of the freedom-loving people of America to the realization that no sooner has a nation been established based on rights, than those rights start to be undermined by elite groups who see no reason to give the people rights. For they want the people to remain as the slaves of the elite.

O Portia, I am confident,
I am a cosmic instrument.
I came to earth from heaven sent,
to help bring forward her ascent.

**O Portia, opportunity,
I am beyond duality.
I focus now internally,
with you I grow eternally.**

Part 3

1. I invoke the awakening of the freedom-loving people of America to the realization that members of the elite have attempted to enslave the people by undermining the democratic institutions and democratic freedoms.

16 | Invoking the true alchemy of freedom

O Saint Germain, you do inspire,
my vision raised forever higher,
with you I form a figure-eight,
your Golden Age I co-create.

**O Saint Germain, what love you bring,
it truly makes all matter sing,
your violet flame does all restore,
with you we are becoming more.**

2. I invoke the awakening of the freedom-loving people of America to the realization that the elite have especially attempted to do this through the money system.

O Saint Germain, what Freedom Flame,
released when we recite your name,
acceleration is your gift,
our planet it will surely lift.

**O Saint Germain, what love you bring,
it truly makes all matter sing,
your violet flame does all restore,
with you we are becoming more.**

3. I invoke the awakening of the freedom-loving people of America to the realization that there were international bankers who financed the British in the Revolutionary War, and even found ways to finance the revolutionary forces.

O Saint Germain, in love we claim,
our right to bring your violet flame,
from you Above, to us below,
it is an all-transforming flow.

> O Saint Germain, what love you bring,
> it truly makes all matter sing,
> your violet flame does all restore,
> with you we are becoming more.

4. I invoke the awakening of the freedom-loving people of America to the realization that not long after George Washington's presidency was over, some of these international bankers managed to write themselves into American government and American life through an unholy bank charter that should never have been given to anyone and was from the start unconstitutional.

> O Saint Germain, I love you so,
> my aura filled with violet glow,
> my chakras filled with violet fire,
> I am your cosmic amplifier.

> **O Saint Germain, what love you bring,**
> **it truly makes all matter sing,**
> **your violet flame does all restore,**
> **with you we are becoming more.**

5. I invoke the awakening of the freedom-loving people of America to the realization that up to very recent times, these bankers have managed to deceive the government into letting the people once again guarantee the loans from the elite with their life-blood, with their labor, which is all they have to give.

> O Saint Germain, I am now free,
> your violet flame is therapy,
> transform all hang-ups in my mind,
> as inner peace I surely find.

**O Saint Germain, what love you bring,
it truly makes all matter sing,
your violet flame does all restore,
with you we are becoming more.**

6. I invoke the awakening of the freedom-loving people of America to the realization that we are moving towards a point where the people are faced with the inevitable situation of either no employment or higher prices on necessities.

O Saint Germain, my body pure,
your violet flame for all is cure,
consume the cause of all disease,
and therefore I am all at ease.

**O Saint Germain, what love you bring,
it truly makes all matter sing,
your violet flame does all restore,
with you we are becoming more.**

7. I invoke the awakening of the freedom-loving people of America to the realization that either the economy must become so bad that people can no longer feed their families, or we must educate ourselves about the economy and the financial system.

O Saint Germain, I'm karma-free,
the past no longer burdens me,
a brand new opportunity,
I am in Christic unity.

> **O Saint Germain, what love you bring,**
> **it truly makes all matter sing,**
> **your violet flame does all restore,**
> **with you we are becoming more.**

8. I invoke the awakening of the freedom-loving people of America to the realization that we need to see how money is being used to create a slavery that might not appear as slavery, but it truly binds the people as much as the feudal societies where no peasant was allowed to move away from the land of the landlord to which he belonged.

> O Saint Germain, we are now one,
> I am for you a violet sun,
> as we transform this planet earth,
> your Golden Age is given birth.

> **O Saint Germain, what love you bring,**
> **it truly makes all matter sing,**
> **your violet flame does all restore,**
> **with you we are becoming more.**

9. I invoke the awakening of the freedom-loving people of America to the realization that the American people cannot in many cases move away from their homes that belong to the mortgage companies. For they have no way of selling the homes for a price anywhere near what they owe on them.

> O Saint Germain, the earth is free,
> from burden of duality,
> in oneness we bring what is best,
> your Golden Age is manifest.

> **O Saint Germain, what love you bring,**
> **it truly makes all matter sing,**
> **your violet flame does all restore,**
> **with you we are becoming more.**

Part 4

1. I invoke the awakening of the freedom-loving people of America to the realization that it is necessary to consider: "To whom do we owe this money?" Who owns the debt? Where does the debt come from? Who is collecting the interest off the debt?

> O Portia, in your own retreat,
> with Mother's Love you do me greet.
> As all my tests I now complete,
> old patterns I no more repeat.

> **O Portia, opportunity,**
> **I am beyond duality.**
> **I focus now internally,**
> **with you I grow eternally.**

2. I invoke the awakening of the freedom-loving people of America to the realization that the debt is backed by the government but does the government collect the interest? Nay, the private banks of the power elite collect the interest.

O Portia, Justice is your name,
upholding Cosmic Honor Flame,
No longer will I play the game,
of seeking to remain the same.

**O Portia, opportunity,
I am beyond duality.
I focus now internally,
with you I grow eternally.**

3. I invoke the awakening of the freedom-loving people of America to the realization that there is a need to revolutionize the entire system, and say that when real estate prices were artificially raised and now have collapsed, then it is no longer right that the people should owe an artificial debt.

O Portia, in the cosmic flow,
one with you, I ever grow.
I am the chalice here below,
of cosmic justice you bestow.

**O Portia, opportunity,
I am beyond duality.
I focus now internally,
with you I grow eternally.**

4. I invoke the awakening of the freedom-loving people of America to the realization that the debt on a house should be reflected by the market value of that property and not some previous artificially created bubble value that has nothing to do with anything real.

16 | Invoking the true alchemy of freedom

O Portia, cosmic balance bring,
eternal hope, my heart does sing.
Protected by your Mother's wing,
I feel at one with everything.

**O Portia, opportunity,
I am beyond duality.
I focus now internally,
with you I grow eternally.**

5. I invoke the Flame of Freedom to challenge the assumptions, the mental boxes, that have created the current situation where there is not only gridlock in the Capitol building, but there is gridlock in the Supreme Court, there is gridlock in the financial system, there is gridlock in the economy.

O Portia, bring the Mother Light,
to set all free from darkest night.
Your Love Flame shines forever bright,
with Saint Germain now hold me tight.

**O Portia, opportunity,
I am beyond duality.
I focus now internally,
with you I grow eternally.**

6. I invoke the awakening of the freedom-loving people of America to the realization that the power elite, in their fear of a free economy, have attempted to clamp down on the financial system so that money cannot flow freely.

O Portia, in your mastery,
I feel transforming chemistry.
In your light of reality,
I find the golden alchemy.

O Portia, opportunity,
I am beyond duality.
I focus now internally,
with you I grow eternally.

7. I invoke the awakening of the freedom-loving people of America to the realization that when money cannot flow freely, it cannot be multiplied and the economy cannot grow.

O Portia, in the cosmic stream,
I am awake from human dream.
Removing now the ego's beam,
I earn my place on cosmic team.

O Portia, opportunity,
I am beyond duality.
I focus now internally,
with you I grow eternally.

8. I invoke the awakening of the freedom-loving people of America to the realization that we cannot force an economy to grow, and the power elite know this. They do not want to force the economy to grow, for they fear economic growth.

O Portia, you come from afar,
you are a cosmic avatar.
So infinite your repertoire,
you are for earth a guiding star.

**O Portia, opportunity,
I am beyond duality.
I focus now internally,
with you I grow eternally.**

9. I invoke the awakening of the freedom-loving people of America to the realization that the elite know that they cannot control it when the economy is growing beyond a certain level.

O Portia, I am confident,
I am a cosmic instrument.
I came to earth from heaven sent,
to help bring forward her ascent.

**O Portia, opportunity,
I am beyond duality.
I focus now internally,
with you I grow eternally.**

Part 5

1. I invoke the awakening of the freedom-loving people of America to the realization that the elite seek to maintain economic growth below a certain level—and when they cannot, they panic and then they precipitate a crisis that then crashes the economy. And then they feel they again have some control.

O Saint Germain, you do inspire,
my vision raised forever higher,
with you I form a figure-eight,
your Golden Age I co-create.

> **O Saint Germain, what love you bring,**
> **it truly makes all matter sing,**
> **your violet flame does all restore,**
> **with you we are becoming more.**

2. I invoke the awakening of the freedom-loving people of America to the realization that this is the cycle of inflated growth and then inflated non-growth, inflated collapse, that we have seen in the American economy almost from the beginning.

> O Saint Germain, what Freedom Flame,
> released when we recite your name,
> acceleration is your gift,
> our planet it will surely lift.

> **O Saint Germain, what love you bring,**
> **it truly makes all matter sing,**
> **your violet flame does all restore,**
> **with you we are becoming more.**

3. I invoke the awakening of the freedom-loving people of America to the realization that this will only accelerate, unless we stand up to it and say: "No more! We will not accept, that the money system in these United States is not controlled by Congress, who are elected and who are constitutionally authorized to do so. We will no longer tolerate this, and therefore we do not want the Federal Reserve to be in control of the money system. We demand that Congress takes back its constitutional power as the only authority that has the right to print money."

> O Saint Germain, in love we claim,
> our right to bring your violet flame,
> from you Above, to us below,
> it is an all-transforming flow.

> **O Saint Germain, what love you bring,**
> **it truly makes all matter sing,**
> **your violet flame does all restore,**
> **with you we are becoming more.**

4. I invoke the awakening of the freedom-loving people of America to the realization that we need to be willing to rethink, to reeducate ourselves, to let our old sense that "all is well with the American Dream" die.

> O Saint Germain, I love you so,
> my aura filled with violet glow,
> my chakras filled with violet fire,
> I am your cosmic amplifier.

> **O Saint Germain, what love you bring,**
> **it truly makes all matter sing,**
> **your violet flame does all restore,**
> **with you we are becoming more.**

5. I invoke the awakening of the freedom-loving people of America to the realization that America can be reborn only when the people's vision of America is reborn and is no longer trapped in these old mental boxes created by the power elite.

O Saint Germain, I am now free,
your violet flame is therapy,
transform all hang-ups in my mind,
as inner peace I surely find.

**O Saint Germain, what love you bring,
it truly makes all matter sing,
your violet flame does all restore,
with you we are becoming more.**

6. I call for the Freedom Flame to descend and take command of the American Nation, so that those who are the enemies of freedom can no longer hide and will be challenged to choose life or to choose death—for there is nothing in between.

O Saint Germain, my body pure,
your violet flame for all is cure,
consume the cause of all disease,
and therefore I am all at ease.

**O Saint Germain, what love you bring,
it truly makes all matter sing,
your violet flame does all restore,
with you we are becoming more.**

7. I invoke the awakening of the freedom-loving people of America to the realization that we may not think we are enslaved, because we have fooled ourselves to think that we still live in a free nation.

16 | Invoking the true alchemy of freedom

O Saint Germain, I'm karma-free,
the past no longer burdens me,
a brand new opportunity,
I am in Christic unity.

**O Saint Germain, what love you bring,
it truly makes all matter sing,
your violet flame does all restore,
with you we are becoming more.**

8. I invoke the awakening of the freedom-loving people of America to the realization that we can fool ourselves into being able to overlook encroachments upon our freedom so that we still maintain a sense of equilibrium that we are a free nation.

O Saint Germain, we are now one,
I am for you a violet sun,
as we transform this planet earth,
your Golden Age is given birth.

**O Saint Germain, what love you bring,
it truly makes all matter sing,
your violet flame does all restore,
with you we are becoming more.**

9. I call to all Americans: "Wake up NOW and recognize that we are no longer a free nation, and that we have not been a free nation for a very long time. Wake up now and claim your true freedom. Reach for the vision of true freedom. Claim it, and then be willing to demand that your government embodies it."

O Saint Germain, the earth is free,
from burden of duality,
in oneness we bring what is best,
your Golden Age is manifest.

**O Saint Germain, what love you bring,
it truly makes all matter sing,
your violet flame does all restore,
with you we are becoming more.**

Part 6

1. I call to all Americans: "Take a stand for life! For right now you are not even taking a stand for death. You are sitting down, you are sleeping on your watch. You have been lulled asleep by the good life, but you do not see that the good life is crumbling around you."

O Portia, in your own retreat,
with Mother's Love you do me greet.
As all my tests I now complete,
old patterns I no more repeat.

**O Portia, opportunity,
I am beyond duality.
I focus now internally,
with you I grow eternally.**

2. I call to all Americans: "Take heed and wake up before the chaos can no longer be turned back." One way or another, change will come. One way or another, this nation will achieve

greater freedom economically and in any other way. For there is no other way to bring the Golden Age than to break down the prison walls that are holding back change.

O Portia, Justice is your name,
upholding Cosmic Honor Flame,
No longer will I play the game,
of seeking to remain the same.

**O Portia, opportunity,
I am beyond duality.
I focus now internally,
with you I grow eternally.**

3. Change will come. The Flame of Freedom makes change inevitable. There is no way to stop this, there is no power on earth – neither the power elite, nor even the will of the majority of the people – that can stop this.

O Portia, in the cosmic flow,
one with you, I ever grow.
I am the chalice here below,
of cosmic justice you bestow.

**O Portia, opportunity,
I am beyond duality.
I focus now internally,
with you I grow eternally.**

4. I invoke the awakening of the freedom-loving people of America to the realization that there are enough people in embodiment who have gone close to or beyond the 96th level of consciousness and who have demanded greater freedom.

> O Portia, cosmic balance bring,
> eternal hope, my heart does sing.
> Protected by your Mother's wing,
> I feel at one with everything.
>
> **O Portia, opportunity,**
> **I am beyond duality.**
> **I focus now internally,**
> **with you I grow eternally.**

5. I invoke the awakening of the freedom-loving people of America to the realization that when we come together in sufficient numbers, we can actually outweigh the will of the majority. And this is how we have true self-government.

> O Portia, bring the Mother Light,
> to set all free from darkest night.
> Your Love Flame shines forever bright,
> with Saint Germain now hold me tight.
>
> **O Portia, opportunity,**
> **I am beyond duality.**
> **I focus now internally,**
> **with you I grow eternally.**

6. I invoke the awakening of the freedom-loving people of America to the realization that the power elite – and even the government apparatus that is out of touch with freedom – must be forced to see the handwriting on the wall.

16 | Invoking the true alchemy of freedom

> O Portia, in your mastery,
> I feel transforming chemistry.
> In your light of reality,
> I find the golden alchemy.
>
> **O Portia, opportunity,**
> **I am beyond duality.**
> **I focus now internally,**
> **with you I grow eternally.**

7. I invoke the awakening of the freedom-loving people of America to the realization that those who rule have to make concessions, they have to change the system they have created, they have to step down from their self-created pedestals that are elevated above the people.

> O Portia, in the cosmic stream,
> I am awake from human dream.
> Removing now the ego's beam,
> I earn my place on cosmic team.
>
> **O Portia, opportunity,**
> **I am beyond duality.**
> **I focus now internally,**
> **with you I grow eternally.**

8. I say with Saint Germain: "I AM the Flame of Freedom! I AM Saint Germain, and I AM here to see this change through to the golden age vision that I AM! I do not hold a vision as an external vision; I embody it as the true alchemist.

O Portia, you come from afar,
you are a cosmic avatar.
So infinite your repertoire,
you are for earth a guiding star.

**O Portia, opportunity,
I am beyond duality.
I focus now internally,
with you I grow eternally.**

9. I say with Saint Germain: "I have become the Golden Age! I AM the Golden Age! Lock in to my Presence, that you may be the Golden Age here below as I AM the Golden Age Above. As Above, So below. You and I: One. Out of the One: Many. Out of the Many: One. This is alchemy, and I AM here!"

O Portia, I am confident,
I am a cosmic instrument.
I came to earth from heaven sent,
to help bring forward her ascent.

**O Portia, opportunity,
I am beyond duality.
I focus now internally,
with you I grow eternally.**

Sealing

In the name of the I AM THAT I AM, I accept that Archangel Michael, Astrea and Shiva form an impenetrable shield around myself and all constructive people, sealing us from all fear-based energies in all four octaves. I accept that the Light of God is consuming and transforming all fear-based energies that make up the dark forces working against America!

17 | WHAT IT TAKES TO BE A GOOD PRESIDENT OF THE UNITED STATES

This dictation was given at Mount Vernon, which was George Washington's personal estate in Virginia. Georg Washington was one of the incarnations of the Ascended Master Godfre.

I AM the Ascended Master Godfre, and I welcome you to the grounds of this historical national landmark, which used to be my gentleman's estate here in Virginia. Many happy hours were spent here, some of the happiest riding on my horses, alone or accompanied only by my personal attendant—who was not to me a piece of property but was a trusted friend, truly also seeing himself as such.

Nevertheless, was there not an amazingly sharp divide back then between different groups of people? You may look at this nation and see the divide between slaves and free men, but there were many other divisions in American society. Divisions that truly, from the very outset, formed the greatest threat to the establishment of this nation, to the survival of this nation. Even today, they form the greatest threat to the ongoingness and the acceleration of this nation towards its golden age potential.

Establishing the United States without bloodshed?

Thus, it was in this place that I was able to withdraw somewhat from this divided, fragmented, dualistic society and the ongoing dualistic struggle—that was such a big part of my life in that embodiment as George Washington. Truly, even from a young age, I was brought into this dualistic struggle by serving in the British army, and – during the revolutionary war – just another phase of this struggle.

Thus, when I had occasion to walk or ride on this property, I would sometimes contemplate a question, which very few Americans today bother to think about. It was the question of how we might have achieved nationhood without the spilling of blood. Would it have been possible indeed to establish the United States of America as a free independent nation without the revolutionary war?

Certainly, at the time I could not see how. Neither could Jefferson or any of the other Founding Fathers. Even though many of the so-called Founding Fathers of this nation had a background in freemasonry – and therefore believed in universal spiritual principles and Divine providence – we still were not able to see how we could achieve greater independence from England without incurring the wrath of the King and the subsequent military clampdown that was – or at least seemed – inevitable in those days.

You, who have grown up in societies or in a time when there was less warfare – or at least without being directly involved with it yourself – will find it difficult to understand the mindset back then where armed conflict was such an almost natural part of life. It was often taken for granted that there simply was no other way to work out solutions to what seemed like major conflicts.

Yet, of course, when you look back with the perspective of an ascended master, you can begin to see just how many opportunities there were for actually having forged a separate nation. When you look today, you can see that had a different course been set, there would still have been an independent nation on the North American continent today. It would surely have taken longer; it would not have been established when the United States of America was established. Yet, it would have been there today. In the process of pursuing a peaceful transformation, England itself would also have been transformed faster than it otherwise was.

The eagerness for armed conflict

Of course, hindsight is always 20/20, as they say. Nevertheless, there is always validity in looking at and learning from the lessons of history. Back then, we were – those of us who started the process of independence and fought in the revolutionary war – not only quick to call for armed uprising, we were eager for it. For we saw it as a decisive way to further our own careers, even our sense of personal honor and pride.

This is a mindset that most of the spiritual people of today will find alien to the way they have grown up. But that is because so much has happened in the collective consciousness of humankind since then. You have been fortunate to grow up in a part of the world where the collective consciousness is not as steeped in conflict as it is in certain other areas.

Look, for example, to the Middle East or Africa or other parts of the globe where there is much more tension and conflict. Consider that the mindset in which I grew up as George Washington, was fairly similar in some ways to what you see in the world today. People are ready to engage in conflict, almost at a moment's notice, because it is always there as an underlying reality in their world view. They see it not only as inevitable, they see it as desirable for a variety of reasons.

The young George Washington

I was born in a not wealthy family in that lifetime, but a family that had ambitions. Even though my father died early, I had absorbed enough of the consciousness that he embodied, the ambition to improve his status in society and become somebody. This was, of course, a mindset that was unique to the colonies, for in Europe people were born into certain stations and most of them would die in the same stations. Here in the United States, there was a new consciousness (even though it was not the United States at the time but the colonies) of realizing that you could improve your station in life.

You could be born in a relatively poor family, and you could climb the social ladder and achieve status. Of course, this could not be done if you were a slave. But if you were born free, then you had this opportunity, through your skill and initiative and your willingness to take a risk. Thus, if you look at the young George Washington, you will clearly see that kind of mentality. I wanted to achieve in my life what my father had not achieved in his, and I was willing to take a risk to achieve it by joining the armed forces, as that was one of the ways to improve your status back then. So, I joined. I threw myself into the uncertainty of armed conflict, and I learned many lessons that became valuable to me, not only in my role as leader during the revolutionary war but about life in general. How fragile it is, how easily it is lost to those who are not, as I came to see it, favored by Divine providence. For there were battles where I saw my friends die around me and where I had bullets flying through my coats—and yet I escaped unharmed.

I knew – I had a growing realization within me – that it could only have been Divine providence that spared my life, because I was selected by that Divine providence for some greater mission. Of course, not knowing what it was when I was young, but it became gradually clearer as I grew into a position in the revolutionary war and eventually, of course, as President.

You see, then, how I started as a young man, having little regard for the lives of others, being willing to further my own personal career by essentially having an occupation that required me to take the lives of other people. This was simply the mindset of the time: kill or be killed, an eye for an eye and a tooth for a tooth, whatever was required to prove your valor in battle.

The maturing George Washington

Yet, a change began to happen in my consciousness during the revolutionary war. Especially in that winter at Valley Forge where I was beyond the brink of complete despair, coming to a point where I completely gave up all personal ambition, all personal desire, all personal expectations of what life should be.

I came to the exact same point that this messenger has described before he started the AskRealJesus website, of saying, literally, to God: "You can take me home right now!" I knew that if I had died at that moment, I would have had no regrets, I would have been willing to leave everything in that lifetime behind in order to move on to some other service.

I truly realized that I of my own self could do nothing. There was no way that I alone – with my leadership and with the men I had at my disposal – could win this war for a new nation. All of my youthful ambitions had made me believe that I had the skills to lead. My early victories had made me even more sure that one day I would eventually triumph and my personal ambitions to achieve the highest standards would be fulfilled, through my bold choice to lead this nation. Yet on my knees at Valley Forge, I gave it all up. I gave it all up, my beloved. I surrendered myself entirely unto God as I saw it, the God of nature, the God within, and I commended my life and my spirit to that higher Being. Which at the time I sensed, but could not name as the I AM Presence, as Saint Germain later did through me in my role as messenger for him.

From that moment on, the young George Washington effectively died. There, in the cold dark days in that distant forest, he died. Yet, *I* did not die. I was not taken home. I realized that there could only be one reason why I was still in embodiment, and it was that Divine providence still had some role for me to play. Divine providence had something it wanted to do through me, now that I had gotten myself out of the way, my own ambition out of the way.

Not wanting to be king

So, I was reborn. Thus came, of course, the process that eventually led to the surrender of the British and the formation of a new nation. This, then, led to the crucial situation where I stood there – as the hero of the new nation – and I was offered, basically, the highest possible power. I could have taken that power, as Napoleon took it. Yet, I declined, and this was the pivotal moment in my embodiment in the public life.

Had it not been for my total surrender in that distant valley, I could never have given up the trappings of power. They surely were pulling at me with all of their might, to get me to take the position as a god for this new nation, thereby thinking that I could do this. Nevertheless, because of my previous surrender, I knew that I could not be a king or an emperor for this new nation. Thus, I was able to once again surrender and decline this position. This was indeed what made it possible for me to then later accept the position as the first President of the United States, and conduct that position in a way that I would have never been able to do before this total surrender to God.

How to be a good President

Thus, what is the moral of telling you this story? For surely, it is not to lament about my personal experiences that have long been transcended in the ascension fires. It is indeed to show you what it takes to be a good President of these United States. It is precisely this one quality: the total surrender to a higher power. The absolute, uncompromising acceptance that you can of your own self do nothing, even though they say you are holding the most powerful office in the world.

You need to be able to stand in front of a mirror, look yourself straight in the eyes and accept: "I am nothing, I can do nothing without a higher power. I can only be successful as President by being the open door, a clear pane of glass." Thus, this is the key to being a successful President. This is why I could say that eight years was enough, and thus set a precedent for this nation that otherwise could easily have been broken by those who had not surrendered their desire for ultimate power—and thus could, even at an early stage, have transformed this nation back towards a more totalitarian form of government.

This, then, is the lesson to learn from the life of George Washington: the surrender onto a higher power. The powers of men may seem intoxicating when you have them in such a measure that you think nothing on earth could take it away from you. But I tell you, there is no amount of power that can preserve you when Divine providence decides to turn the wheels of destiny.

There is nothing that can stop the wheels of time from taking away anything and everything you think you can own and possess on this earth. Thus, only those who know this, will be able to surrender and let go, whereas those who do not know will continue to use whatever power they have available to them, until their ultimate defeat, as you saw with Hitler, Napoleon, many other people throughout the ages. Even people who have not been leaders of nations, but who have continued doing the same thing over and over again, thinking that one day they would surely mount enough force to get a different result.

Practical realism

You see, when you surrender yourself entirely unto God, you realize a very simple thing: we live in a universe that has certain mechanical properties. What you send into the cosmic mirror, the mirror will reflect back to you. The harder the impulse you send out, the harder the reflection coming back. If you think that fighting your own reflection requires you to use more force, you only get an even stronger reflection coming back. This can go on until you are either broken or until you see the light and just give it up, give up the entire dualistic game. This, then, is indeed the quality that needs to be manifest, if you are to be a successful leader of this nation or any democratic nation. Even though democracy must be secular and must not be taken over by a particular religion, a democracy cannot function without the acceptance of a higher power, a higher principle, a higher idea.

Nevertheless, I am not thereby saying that in order to be a successful President of the United States, you have to be an idealist. For if you look at my life as George Washington, you will see that even though I clearly had ideals and principles, I was not what you would call an idealist. If you look at my consciousness during the revolutionary war, you will clearly see that I was a practical realist. I used what I had available to me, and I attempted to multiply it, to gain the maximum effect. Then, when I acknowledged the fact that I would not have more troops, I would not have more gun powder, I would not have more money, then I committed myself one hundred percent to doing the best that could be done, and then accepting the result.

The alpha is the total surrender to God, the omega is the practical realism of what is possible in the material universe. This is also why I was not able to find a solution to the slavery issue that you clearly see outpictured here at Mount Vernon. Yet you will see that even the man who was a greater idealist, such as my friend Thomas, could not resolve the issue either through his reasoning faculties. This was, again in hindsight, partly because of the collective consciousness of the time. It was too difficult for us to see through the fog of the collective consciousness and do what needed to be done to end slavery, at least on a personal basis. I was too focused on the practical aspects, of not wanting to break up slave families. Yet, had I been more willing to surrender entirely unto God in this issue as well, then I would have found the solution. So you see, the total surrender unto God is not a one-time process; it is something that is required every time you face an issue where you seemingly cannot solve an enigma, solve a problem.

George Washington's law

My beloved, let me give you George Washington's law: If you do not see a solution to a problem, it is because there is something you have not surrendered. You have not attained total surrender with regards to this issue, for otherwise the solution would become obvious.

This, then, is a rule that you might find occasion to ponder, as you pursue spiritual growth and thereby become the people in today's age who will have, potentially, an even greater impact on the collective consciousness by setting examples that go beyond the example I set as George Washington or that was set by the Founding Fathers. For truly, this is a new day and a new age.

So many young people come to this Mount Vernon estate and museum, and they look at the life of George Washington and they think that they should somehow follow my example. But times have moved on. It is no longer the highest solution that this nation of the United States is engaged in conflicts around the world. Therefore, it still finds it necessary to educate its young people – to program them – to think they have to fight for freedom, as you find in several museums in this nation's capital and even here. This is no longer the highest possible example, and thus there is a need for those who will set a new example, a higher example based on the collective consciousness as it is today and the potential for a Golden Age.

You who are open to a universal spiritual teaching – as I was open by becoming a Freemason in my early years – you are the ones who have the potential to set a higher example in this age. You can learn certain lessons from studying my life as George Washington. But again, you must, of course, go beyond. You must surrender your expectations and graven images as I surrendered mine when I was kneeling in my tent on that cold winter day where it seemed like the cause of forging a new nation was lost beyond repair. Nothing is ever lost for God. It is only for the human consciousness that it can seem as if something is lost. Thus, when you think all is lost, it is because there is a part of your human consciousness that you have not surrendered, and it is this consciousness that thinks all is lost.

What is lost is only your unreal expectations. When you surrender those unreal expectations, you will be reborn into a higher vision where you see that nothing was truly lost, for everything was a transformation. Had we lost that revolutionary war, there would still have been a free nation on this continent. Again, it would have taken longer, but as even democracy was eventually established in England – and India and Canada gained their independence – you could see that, surely, the American colonies could have achieved the same in time.

Thus, there is a time to take leadership, and there is a time to lay down the leadership. There is a time to take arms, and there is a time to lay down your arms and grab the plow. Wise are those who know the timing. I am not hereby saying that I or others in the revolutionary war should not have done what we did. This is not a point of going back and rewriting history. It is a matter of realizing that there was an alternative to what we did. At the time, it was not a possible or practical alternative, given the state of consciousness we had and the collective state of consciousness and physical conditions.

My point is that you cannot today look back at the Founding Fathers and the revolutionary war and say that you today should do what we did back then. You should be inspired by our example, but you should transcend the example, surrender your own expectations and graven images and grasp the higher vision for what is the practical solution today.

Thus, with a fond gaze over these grounds where I had such a sense of peace in my later years, I seal this release. I give my gratitude to the person who has been willing to be the open door, allowing me to anchor a portion, not of the flame of George Washington but the flame of the Ascended Master Godfre here on these grounds. So that those who come here from now on may indeed be inspired to reach for the higher vision and to understand the need for the total surrender before that higher vision can be grasped. Thus, Godfre I AM, and this is my flame.

18 | INVOKING A HIGHER VISION OF THE PRESIDENCY

In the name of the I AM THAT I AM, Jesus Christ, I use the authority that I have as a being in embodiment on earth to call upon Godfree to reinforce my calls and use my chakras to project the statements in this invocation into the collective consciousness and awaken Americans to a higher vision for what it means to be President. Awaken Americans to the reality that we are spiritual beings and that we can co-create a new future by working with the ascended masters. I especially call for ...

[Make your own calls here.]

Part 1

1. I invoke the awakening of the freedom-loving people of America to the realization that the many divisions in American society from the very outset formed

the greatest threat to the establishment of this nation, to the survival of this nation.

> O Godfre, your ascension light,
> leads us through the darkest night,
> it is a trail that you have carved,
> for all who are for freedom starved.

> **O Godfre, I am free to be,**
> **one with God and one with thee,**
> **there is no greater love I see,**
> **than what I feel for God in me.**

2. I invoke the awakening of the freedom-loving people of America to the realization that even today, these divisions form the greatest threat to the ongoingness and the acceleration of this nation towards its golden age potential.

> O Godfre, I surrender all,
> as I now follow inner call.
> The providence that is Divine,
> will show me plan uniquely mine.

> **O Godfre, I am free to be,**
> **one with God and one with thee,**
> **there is no greater love I see,**
> **than what I feel for God in me.**

3. I invoke the awakening of the freedom-loving people of America to the realization that we need to contemplate the question of how we might have achieved nationhood without the spilling of blood.

18 | Invoking a higher vision of the presidency

> O Godfre, show me how to be,
> from man's ambitions clearly free.
> I can of my self nothing do,
> and this I want to learn from you.
>
> **O Godfre, I am free to be,**
> **one with God and one with thee,**
> **there is no greater love I see,**
> **than what I feel for God in me.**

4. I invoke the awakening of the freedom-loving people of America to the realization that we need to consider if it would have been possible to establish the United States of America as a free independent nation without the revolutionary war?

> O Godfre, I would know your flame,
> so I will never be the same.
> I want to grow forever more,
> and help God's kingdom to restore.
>
> **O Godfre, I am free to be,**
> **one with God and one with thee,**
> **there is no greater love I see,**
> **than what I feel for God in me.**

5. I invoke the awakening of the freedom-loving people of America to the realization that the Founding Fathers were not able to see how they could achieve greater independence from England without incurring the wrath of the King and the subsequent military clampdown that seemed inevitable.

O Godfre, help me now to see,
complete surrender is the key.
All problems can be solved by me,
when I surrender all to thee.

**O Godfre, I am free to be,
one with God and one with thee,
there is no greater love I see,
than what I feel for God in me.**

6. I invoke the awakening of the freedom-loving people of America to the realization that there were many opportunities for forging a separate nation.

O Godfre, for your flame I call,
a great example to us all.
You stand so firm in time of need,
so we can move with true God-speed.

**O Godfre, I am free to be,
one with God and one with thee,
there is no greater love I see,
than what I feel for God in me.**

7. I invoke the awakening of the freedom-loving people of America to the realization that had a different course been set, there would still have been an independent nation on the North American continent today.

O Godfre, I would know your mind,
to see the secret you did find.
of when to do and when to stop,
so I am always going up.

**O Godfre, I am free to be,
one with God and one with thee,
there is no greater love I see,
than what I feel for God in me.**

8. I invoke the awakening of the freedom-loving people of America to the realization that it would have taken longer, but it would have been there today, and in the process of pursuing a peaceful transformation, England itself would also have been transformed faster than it otherwise was.

O Godfre, you are always free,
for you obedience is the key,
we go beyond all human flaw,
by following the greater law.

**O Godfre, I am free to be,
one with God and one with thee,
there is no greater love I see,
than what I feel for God in me.**

9. I invoke the awakening of the freedom-loving people of America to the realization that people back then were not only quick to call for armed uprising, they were eager for it. They saw it as a decisive way to further their own careers, even their sense of personal honor and pride.

O Godfre, light is shining clear,
the mighty I AM Presence near,
I go with you beyond the fray,
to set example in my day.

**O Godfre, I am free to be,
one with God and one with thee,
there is no greater love I see,
than what I feel for God in me.**

Part 2

1. I invoke the awakening of the freedom-loving people of America to the realization that even today, many people are ready to engage in conflict because it is always there as an underlying reality in their world view. They see it not only as inevitable, they see it as desirable for a variety of reasons.

O Godfre, your ascension light,
leads us through the darkest night,
it is a trail that you have carved,
for all who are for freedom starved.

**O Godfre, I am free to be,
one with God and one with thee,
there is no greater love I see,
than what I feel for God in me.**

2. I invoke the awakening of the freedom-loving people of America to the realization that the young George Washington was filled with ambition and was willing to join the armed forces, and kill other people in order to further his ambitions.

18 | Invoking a higher vision of the presidency

O Godfre, I surrender all,
as I now follow inner call.
The providence that is Divine,
will show me plan uniquely mine.

O Godfre, I am free to be,
one with God and one with thee,
there is no greater love I see,
than what I feel for God in me.

3. I invoke the awakening of the freedom-loving people of America to the realization that during the winter at Valley Forge, George Washington came to a point where he completely gave up all personal ambitions, all personal desires, all personal expectations of what life should be.

O Godfre, show me how to be,
from man's ambitions clearly free.
I can of my self nothing do,
and this I want to learn from you.

O Godfre, I am free to be,
one with God and one with thee,
there is no greater love I see,
than what I feel for God in me.

4. I invoke the awakening of the freedom-loving people of America to the realization that he came to the point of saying to God: "You can take me home right now!" If he had died at that moment, he would have had no regrets, he would have been willing to leave everything in that lifetime behind in order to move on to some other service.

> O Godfre, I would know your flame,
> so I will never be the same.
> I want to grow forever more,
> and help God's kingdom to restore.
>
> **O Godfre, I am free to be,**
> **one with God and one with thee,**
> **there is no greater love I see,**
> **than what I feel for God in me.**

5. I invoke the awakening of the freedom-loving people of America to the realization that he, of his own self, could do nothing. There was no way that he alone could win this war for a new nation.

> O Godfre, help me now to see,
> complete surrender is the key.
> All problems can be solved by me,
> when I surrender all to thee.
>
> **O Godfre, I am free to be,**
> **one with God and one with thee,**
> **there is no greater love I see,**
> **than what I feel for God in me.**

6. I invoke the awakening of the freedom-loving people of America to the realization that he surrendered himself entirely unto God as he saw it, the God of nature, the God within, and he commended his life and his spirit to that higher being.

18 | Invoking a higher vision of the presidency

O Godfre, for your flame I call,
a great example to us all.
You stand so firm in time of need,
so we can move with true God-speed.

O Godfre, I am free to be,
one with God and one with thee,
there is no greater love I see,
than what I feel for God in me.

7. I invoke the awakening of the freedom-loving people of America to the realization that from that moment on, the young George Washington effectively died. Yet he was reborn into a new sense of mission.

O Godfre, I would know your mind,
to see the secret you did find.
of when to do and when to stop,
so I am always going up.

O Godfre, I am free to be,
one with God and one with thee,
there is no greater love I see,
than what I feel for God in me.

8. I invoke the awakening of the freedom-loving people of America to the realization that when George Washington had won the war and was the hero of the new nation, he was offered the highest possible power.

O Godfre, you are always free,
for you obedience is the key,
we go beyond all human flaw,
by following the greater law.

**O Godfre, I am free to be,
one with God and one with thee,
there is no greater love I see,
than what I feel for God in me.**

9. I invoke the awakening of the freedom-loving people of America to the realization that had it not been for his total surrender, he could never have given up the trappings of power. Yet he was able to once again surrender and decline this position.

O Godfre, light is shining clear,
the mighty I AM Presence near,
I go with you beyond the fray,
to set example in my day.

**O Godfre, I am free to be,
one with God and one with thee,
there is no greater love I see,
than what I feel for God in me.**

Part 3

1. I invoke the awakening of the freedom-loving people of America to the realization that what it takes to be a good President of these United States is this one quality: the total

surrender to a higher power. The absolute, uncompromising acceptance that you can, of your own self, do nothing, even though they say you are holding the most powerful office in the world.

> O Godfre, your ascension light,
> leads us through the darkest night,
> it is a trail that you have carved,
> for all who are for freedom starved.

> **O Godfre, I am free to be,**
> **one with God and one with thee,**
> **there is no greater love I see,**
> **than what I feel for God in me.**

2. I invoke the awakening of the freedom-loving people of America to the realization that as President, you need to be able to stand in front of a mirror, look yourself straight in the eyes and accept: "I am nothing, I can do nothing without a higher power. I can only be successful as President by being the open door, a clear pane of glass."

> O Godfre, I surrender all,
> as I now follow inner call.
> The providence that is Divine,
> will show me plan uniquely mine.

> **O Godfre, I am free to be,**
> **one with God and one with thee,**
> **there is no greater love I see,**
> **than what I feel for God in me.**

3. I invoke the awakening of the freedom-loving people of America to the realization that this is the key to being a successful President. This is why George Washington could say that eight years was enough, and thus set a precedent for this nation.

> O Godfre, show me how to be,
> from man's ambitions clearly free.
> I can of my self nothing do,
> and this I want to learn from you.
>
> **O Godfre, I am free to be,**
> **one with God and one with thee,**
> **there is no greater love I see,**
> **than what I feel for God in me.**

4. I invoke the awakening of the freedom-loving people of America to the realization that the example of George Washington literally saved America from those who had not surrendered their desire for ultimate power—and thus could even at an early stage have transformed this nation back towards a more totalitarian form of government.

> O Godfre, I would know your flame,
> so I will never be the same.
> I want to grow forever more,
> and help God's kingdom to restore.
>
> **O Godfre, I am free to be,**
> **one with God and one with thee,**
> **there is no greater love I see,**
> **than what I feel for God in me.**

18 | Invoking a higher vision of the presidency

5. I invoke the awakening of the freedom-loving people of America to the realization that the lesson to learn from the life of George Washington is the surrender onto a higher power.

> O Godfre, help me now to see,
> complete surrender is the key.
> All problems can be solved by me,
> when I surrender all to thee.
>
> **O Godfre, I am free to be,**
> **one with God and one with thee,**
> **there is no greater love I see,**
> **than what I feel for God in me.**

6. I invoke the awakening of the freedom-loving people of America to the realization that the powers of men may seem intoxicating when you have them in such a measure that you think nothing on earth could take it away from you. Yet no amount of power can preserve you when Divine providence decides to turn the wheels of destiny.

> O Godfre, for your flame I call,
> a great example to us all.
> You stand so firm in time of need,
> so we can move with true God-speed.
>
> **O Godfre, I am free to be,**
> **one with God and one with thee,**
> **there is no greater love I see,**
> **than what I feel for God in me.**

7. I invoke the awakening of the freedom-loving people of America to the realization that there is nothing that can stop

the wheels of time from taking away anything and everything we think we can own and possess on earth.

> O Godfre, I would know your mind,
> to see the secret you did find.
> of when to do and when to stop,
> so I am always going up.

> **O Godfre, I am free to be,**
> **one with God and one with thee,**
> **there is no greater love I see,**
> **than what I feel for God in me.**

8. I invoke the awakening of the freedom-loving people of America to the realization that only those who know this will be able to surrender and let go, whereas those who do not know will continue to use whatever power they have available to them until their ultimate defeat, as we saw with Hitler, Napoleon and many other people throughout the ages.

> O Godfre, you are always free,
> for you obedience is the key,
> we go beyond all human flaw,
> by following the greater law.

> **O Godfre, I am free to be,**
> **one with God and one with thee,**
> **there is no greater love I see,**
> **than what I feel for God in me.**

9. I invoke the awakening of the freedom-loving people of America to the realization that when we surrender ourselves entirely unto God, we realize that we live in a universe that has

certain mechanical properties. What we send into the cosmic mirror, the mirror will reflect back to us.

> O Godfre, light is shining clear,
> the mighty I AM Presence near,
> I go with you beyond the fray,
> to set example in my day.

> **O Godfre, I am free to be,**
> **one with God and one with thee,**
> **there is no greater love I see,**
> **than what I feel for God in me.**

Part 4

1. I invoke the awakening of the freedom-loving people of America to the realization that the harder the impulse we send out, the harder the reflection coming back. This can go on until we are either broken or until we see the light and give up the entire dualistic game.

> O Godfre, your ascension light,
> leads us through the darkest night,
> it is a trail that you have carved,
> for all who are for freedom starved.

> **O Godfre, I am free to be,**
> **one with God and one with thee,**
> **there is no greater love I see,**
> **than what I feel for God in me.**

2. I invoke the awakening of the freedom-loving people of America to the realization that this is the quality that needs to be manifest, if you are to be a successful leader of this nation or any democratic nation.

> O Godfre, I surrender all,
> as I now follow inner call.
> The providence that is Divine,
> will show me plan uniquely mine.

> **O Godfre, I am free to be,**
> **one with God and one with thee,**
> **there is no greater love I see,**
> **than what I feel for God in me.**

3. I invoke the awakening of the freedom-loving people of America to the realization that even though democracy must be secular and must not be taken over by a particular religion, a democracy cannot function without the acceptance of a higher power, a higher principle, a higher idea.

> O Godfre, show me how to be,
> from man's ambitions clearly free.
> I can of my self nothing do,
> and this I want to learn from you.

> **O Godfre, I am free to be,**
> **one with God and one with thee,**
> **there is no greater love I see,**
> **than what I feel for God in me.**

4. I invoke the awakening of the freedom-loving people of America to the realization that a successful President of the

United States is not an idealist. George Washington had ideals and principles, but he was not an idealist, he was a practical realist.

> O Godfre, I would know your flame,
> so I will never be the same.
> I want to grow forever more,
> and help God's kingdom to restore.
>
> **O Godfre, I am free to be,**
> **one with God and one with thee,**
> **there is no greater love I see,**
> **than what I feel for God in me.**

5. I invoke the awakening of the freedom-loving people of America to the realization that Washington used what he had available and attempted to multiply it. Then, he committed himself one hundred percent to doing the best that could be done, and then accepting the result.

> O Godfre, help me now to see,
> complete surrender is the key.
> All problems can be solved by me,
> when I surrender all to thee.
>
> **O Godfre, I am free to be,**
> **one with God and one with thee,**
> **there is no greater love I see,**
> **than what I feel for God in me.**

6. I invoke the awakening of the freedom-loving people of America to the realization that the alpha is the total surrender

to God, the omega is the practical realism of what is possible in the material universe.

> O Godfre, for your flame I call,
> a great example to us all.
> You stand so firm in time of need,
> so we can move with true God-speed.

> **O Godfre, I am free to be,**
> **one with God and one with thee,**
> **there is no greater love I see,**
> **than what I feel for God in me.**

7. I invoke the awakening of the freedom-loving people of America to the realization that total surrender unto God is not a one-time process; it is something that is required every time we face an issue where we seemingly cannot solve an enigma.

> O Godfre, I would know your mind,
> to see the secret you did find.
> of when to do and when to stop,
> so I am always going up.

> **O Godfre, I am free to be,**
> **one with God and one with thee,**
> **there is no greater love I see,**
> **than what I feel for God in me.**

8. I invoke the awakening of the freedom-loving people of America to the realization that this is George Washington's law: If we do not see a solution to a problem, it is because there is something we have not surrendered. We have not attained

total surrender with regards to this issue, for otherwise the solution would become obvious.

> O Godfre, you are always free,
> for you obedience is the key,
> we go beyond all human flaw,
> by following the greater law.

> **O Godfre, I am free to be,**
> **one with God and one with thee,**
> **there is no greater love I see,**
> **than what I feel for God in me.**

9. I invoke the awakening of the freedom-loving people of America to the realization that by pondering this law, we who are the spiritual people can set examples that go beyond the example set by George Washington or the Founding Fathers.

> O Godfre, light is shining clear,
> the mighty I AM Presence near,
> I go with you beyond the fray,
> to set example in my day.

> **O Godfre, I am free to be,**
> **one with God and one with thee,**
> **there is no greater love I see,**
> **than what I feel for God in me.**

Part 5

1. I invoke the awakening of the freedom-loving people of America to the realization that we cannot look at the life of George Washington and think we should follow his example. Times have moved on.

> O Godfre, your ascension light,
> leads us through the darkest night,
> it is a trail that you have carved,
> for all who are for freedom starved.
>
> **O Godfre, I am free to be,**
> **one with God and one with thee,**
> **there is no greater love I see,**
> **than what I feel for God in me.**

2. I invoke the awakening of the freedom-loving people of America to the realization that it is no longer the highest solution that the United States is engaged in conflicts around the world, and therefore finds it necessary to educate its young people – to program them – to think they have to fight for freedom.

> O Godfre, I surrender all,
> as I now follow inner call.
> The providence that is Divine,
> will show me plan uniquely mine.

> O Godfre, I am free to be,
> one with God and one with thee,
> there is no greater love I see,
> than what I feel for God in me.

3. I invoke the awakening of the freedom-loving people of America to the realization that this is no longer the highest possible example, and thus there is a need for those who will set a new example, a higher example, based on the collective consciousness as it is today and the potential for a Golden Age.

> O Godfre, show me how to be,
> from man's ambitions clearly free.
> I can of my self nothing do,
> and this I want to learn from you.

> O Godfre, I am free to be,
> one with God and one with thee,
> there is no greater love I see,
> than what I feel for God in me.

4. I invoke the awakening of the freedom-loving people of America to the realization that those who are open to a universal spiritual teaching have the potential to set a higher example in this age. We can learn certain lessons from studying the life of George Washington, but we must go beyond.

> O Godfre, I would know your flame,
> so I will never be the same.
> I want to grow forever more,
> and help God's kingdom to restore.

> **O Godfre, I am free to be,
> one with God and one with thee,
> there is no greater love I see,
> than what I feel for God in me.**

5. I invoke the awakening of the freedom-loving people of America to the realization that we must surrender our expectations and graven images as Washington surrendered his. Nothing is ever lost for God. It is only for the human consciousness that it can seem as if something is lost.

> O Godfre, help me now to see,
> complete surrender is the key.
> All problems can be solved by me,
> when I surrender all to thee.

> **O Godfre, I am free to be,
> one with God and one with thee,
> there is no greater love I see,
> than what I feel for God in me.**

6. I invoke the awakening of the freedom-loving people of America to the realization that what can be lost is only our unreal expectations. When we surrender them, we will be reborn into a higher vision where we see that nothing was truly lost, for everything was a transformation.

> O Godfre, for your flame I call,
> a great example to us all.
> You stand so firm in time of need,
> so we can move with true God-speed.

18 | Invoking a higher vision of the presidency

**O Godfre, I am free to be,
one with God and one with thee,
there is no greater love I see,
than what I feel for God in me.**

7. I invoke the awakening of the freedom-loving people of America to the realization that there is a time to take leadership, and there is a time to lay down the leadership. There is a time to take arms, and there is a time to lay down arms and grab the plow. Wise are those who know the timing.

O Godfre, I would know your mind,
to see the secret you did find.
of when to do and when to stop,
so I am always going up.

**O Godfre, I am free to be,
one with God and one with thee,
there is no greater love I see,
than what I feel for God in me.**

8. I invoke the awakening of the freedom-loving people of America to the realization that we cannot today look back at the Founding Fathers and the revolutionary war and say that we should do what they did back then. We should be inspired by their example, but we should transcend the example, surrender our own expectations and graven images and grasp the higher vision for what is the practical solution today.

O Godfre, you are always free,
for you obedience is the key,
we go beyond all human flaw,
by following the greater law.

**O Godfre, I am free to be,
one with God and one with thee,
there is no greater love I see,
than what I feel for God in me.**

9. I invoke the flame that the Ascended Master Godfre has anchored at Mount Vernon. I call for those who come here to be inspired to reach for a higher vision and to understand the need for the total surrender before that higher vision can be grasped.

O Godfre, light is shining clear,
the mighty I AM Presence near,
I go with you beyond the fray,
to set example in my day.

**O Godfre, I am free to be,
one with God and one with thee,
there is no greater love I see,
than what I feel for God in me.**

Sealing

In the name of the I AM THAT I AM, I accept that Archangel Michael, Astrea and Shiva form an impenetrable shield around myself and all constructive people, sealing us from all fear-based energies in all four octaves. I accept that the Light of God is consuming and transforming all fear-based energies that make up the dark forces working against America!

19 | A GOLDEN AGE VIEW OF WHAT IT MEANS TO BE PRESIDENT

This dictation was given outside the White House (but at some distance), Washington, D.C.

Gautama I AM, and I come to seal this series of dictations and the releases of light that we have brought forth here in Washington, D.C. Thus, I come to give you the answer to a question that some of you might have formed in your minds, as you read or listened to this series of dictations here in the National Mall in Washington, D.C. For you have heard us give releases at the Lincoln Memorial, at the Jefferson Monument, at the Federal Reserve, at the Washington Monument, at the National Archives, at the Capitol Building and at the Supreme Court and the Library of Congress. Yet if you are somewhat familiar with the layout of Washington, D.C., you might have wondered why we passed by one location that seems like it should have been included on the list.

We have anchored the light that will help this nation transform itself to a higher level, in many of the important locations in the Capitol, but we have not anchored the light in what some would argue is the most important location of all, namely the White House. You might think that I am here to anchor the light in the White House for this release, which is given outside of the President's residence. Nevertheless, I am not here to anchor a flame, as we have done in the other locations. Yet, I am here to explain why we are not anchoring a flame in the White House.

The need for the President to surrender

It is indeed for several reasons, but one of them is, as Godfre has so eloquently explained, that when you are President of the United States, the only way to be successful is to recognize that you cannot govern this nation out of your own power. Thus, you must come to that point of absolute and total surrender to a higher power, as you see it. Whether you see it as this God or that God, or your higher self, or the Great Architect of the Universe or whatever you will want to call this higher power, you need to surrender your human ambition, your human expectations, your human pride that makes you think that you have – somehow – the capacity to run this large and complex nation. A capacity that sets you above most other people.

This is, of course, one of the lies that is easily believed in, once you have been sworn in and it dawns on you that you are now the holder of what many label as "the most powerful office in the world." You might even think you are the most powerful man in the world, as some have thought—and as many among the people would like to think that their President truly is. It

19 | A golden age view of what it means to be President

is easy – if you have any kind of personal pride – to come to believe in this. Of course, if you had no personal ambition, why would you even aspire to the office, given how conditions are today with the political machinery in the United States? For quite frankly, would anyone who had Buddhic attainment, or even Christ attainment, want to put himself through the political machinery of these United States in this age?

Well, surely, he would not want to, but he might do so if the people had reached a level of consciousness where they were able to recognize such a candidate. This, of course, has not yet happened. Thus, what you see is that the people who are attracted to run for office – and who are willing to set aside their lives and give up their privacy forever – are those who have an ambition. And with ambition, of course, comes pride. For when you achieve your ambition, there will be a sense of pride. You will see this in every President. When you look back through the ages, there are very few who have not had this pride. You will see it in the current President, if you look honestly at his demeanor, at his facial expressions, you will see a certain pride. This is not to say that the current President is worse than so many others that you have seen. I am simply pointing out that it, so to speak, goes with the territory. Of course, this pride is precisely what makes you think that you have the ability to govern. This is, therefore, also what blocks you from achieving that total surrender where you are willing to throw yourself on your knees and give up all human, worldly ambitions and expectations and graven images, and simply say to the higher power as you see it: "Show me the way to go, show me how you would act in this situation." This was what Abraham Lincoln was willing to do. It was what George Washington was willing to do. It was what Thomas Jefferson was *not* willing to do. Of course, many other presidents have not been willing to do so either.

Why there is no flame in the White House

Yet, it is precisely this inability or unwillingness to go through this total humility of the complete surrender that is the reason we are not anchoring a flame in the White House. For once we anchor a flame, all who pass through the flame will experience the light. For some it will flush out their darkness, for others it will inspire and uplift them, but there will be an effect.

Thus, what we want for the White House is that as long as the President thinks he has the power to govern, then he must be left alone so that he does not receive the light or the sponsorship from Above as an automatic grant. He only receives it the moment he humbles himself, surrenders, and asks for assistance from Above. When he comes to that point, the assistance will be given in full measure. Until that point, he will literally be on his own power, or on the power of those around him. You see that there will be a horizontal form of government until there is the willingness to reach up for that vertical assistance from Above; until there is a willingness to be the open door, the clear pane of glass so that you can be "here below as Above."

This, of course, is another aspect of what you need to achieve as President, again as Godfre talked about: the practical realism. Well, when you have the personal ambition, you also have – inevitably – a personal value judgment based on a relative dualistic standard. For your ambition is to raise yourself to a certain status, and that can only be done according to a dualistic value judgment.

When you have this pride, you are likely to be deceived into doing things that you think will be good according to your personal ambition—which might be to leave a certain legacy. Thus, you are likely to be deceived into pursuing goals that are simply not realistic from a practical viewpoint because they cannot be achieved, they cannot be manifested, given the state of the collective consciousness and the practical situation that you face as President. This is, then, when you become overly idealistic, wanting to hold on to the mental structure in your mind, the mental image, and wanting, with all the power available to you as President, to force the nation, and even the world, to fit into your mental box.

You lose the practical realism of what is the highest good for the highest number in the given situation. You will not acknowledge what the given situation truly is, for you want the situation to live up to your ideal, to your mental image. In your pride, you will not listen to the advisors around you, or to the media, or to the people, or to foreign heads of state who tell you that your goal, while noble, simply is not realistic. This is another trap of the Office of President of the United States.

Will the United States be an empire or an example?

There is no office that is more difficult to hold in the entire world than that of being President of the United States. This is, of course, because the United States currently has such a dominant position in the world. It can be either the next empire that will attempt to take over the world, or it can be, truly, an example of a nation that will not be an empire, that will not have a king or an emperor. Was it not precisely this example that George Washington set for this nation, when he resigned his military commission and refused to run for a third term as President, refused to be President for life? Do you not see that this is the example that must be understood, that must be upheld even by the current President?

Indeed, it is absolutely necessary that this nation "under God" does not become an empire that pursues a human ambition, the ambition of the power elite who can never get enough power. They will, as Godfre also explained, continue to use the power available to them in a blind pursuit of their goals; their selfish, self-centered goals. What has happened since the time of George Washington is that the power elite – who have attempted to manipulate the United States behind the scenes – have indeed attempted to gradually, and not noticeably, inflate the powers of the President.

How to manipulate the President

Do you not see – if you study the history of this nation – that when the original delegations formulated the division of power between the Presidency, the Congress and the Supreme Court, they gave far-reaching powers to the President. They did this partly because they had in mind a President of the caliber of George Washington who had already shown his willingness to surrender his ambitions relating to exercising power. Thus, they felt comfortable in giving the decisive powers to the President, without limiting them as has indeed been done in many European nations where in some cases they do not even have a President but only a Prime Minister.

Although Washington was able to exercise these powers in a balanced manner, other presidents have not been equally able. Since then, what has happened is that the Office of the President has taken on far greater powers than is healthy. This, of course, was made even worse during the Bush presidency, especially during the so-called covert efforts of the Vice-President, Dick Cheney. He attempted to take the use of Executive Orders and Executive Powers far beyond what is actually constitutional, or at least beyond what is the intention of the Founding Fathers and what is good for the nation. You might ask yourself: Why it is that the power elite have attempted to inflate the Office of the President? Well, is it not simple, my beloved? It is far easier to manipulate one President than to manipulate hundreds of Congressmen or a larger number of Supreme Court judges than the one President.

Can you not see that, throughout history, there are many examples of how – when power was vested in just one person – that person was so easily deceived by his or her personal ambition into making precisely the wrong choices? This is what the power elite knows, and thus they know that if they set up a political machinery that is simply a sorting mechanism – that sorts out those who are not willing to compromise in order to achieve their ambition – well, then they can make sure that anyone elected to the Office of President is willing to compromise in order to achieve his personal ambitions. Thus, they know they can manipulate that individual into making decisions in a crisis situation that are not good for the all.

What has happened since George Washington's time is that the Office of the President has morphed into a position in the collective psyche that is different from what it was back then where they often compared the President to a king or an emperor. Now, the presidency has taken on a life of its own in the American psyche, and they now look to the President as almost a god-like figure who has, they think, unlimited power.

The President is not God

Is that not why you see that people can elect a President who comes into office with a large approval rating, because the people have believed in the promises he made in order to win election? Then, after only a few months in office, the people begin to realize that he has no chance of delivering on his promises and thus his popularity, his approval rating, begins to go down. Does this not show that the American people have been deceived into thinking that the President alone has greater powers than he actually has, even though, as I said, he has greater powers than he should have in a more balanced political system?

The people think that the President can save them from their troubles, for they fail to realize that beyond the divisions of power set up by the Founding Fathers to limit the powers of the President, the greatest limiting power for the President is precisely the collective consciousness. You can have a President – well, in practical terms you cannot have a President with Buddha-like attainment until the collective consciousness has been raised – but even if theoretically you had a President with Buddhic attainment right now, there would still be a limit to what he could do for the nation. For he would not be able to get anything through beyond what the collective consciousness is willing to accept. You see indeed that no President can bring a change that the collective consciousness cannot handle. For the people are not willing to change accordingly, they are not willing to change their state of consciousness based on the changes in the nation.

A new view of the Presidency is needed

Indeed, what is needed – if America is to make the transition into the Golden Age – is that not only the political powers of the President need to be adjusted, but especially the collective view of the President and the Office of the President need to go through a transformation so that people have a more realistic view. They realize that it is not enough for them to go to the polls every four years and elect a new President. If they are not willing to transform their consciousness, to transcend their old mental boxes, well, then it will make no difference that they elect a new President from a different party or a different background.

This is the change that needs to happen, and that is, again, why we are not anchoring a flame over the White House. It is indeed necessary that the Office of the President is taken down in importance. For this to happen, it may indeed be necessary that one or two presidents will suffer some humiliation while in office so that not only the presidents might learn the lesson of humility, but that the nation might have an opportunity to learn. It can begin to realize that the President is not God, but that the President has the potential to be the open door for God—if indeed he is willing to go through that total surrender and become a clear pane of glass.

I can tell you that in order to be a successful President of the United States, you need to have a great momentum on the 8th Ray of Integration. Of course, you get that only, as I have explained before, by first gaining momentum passing the initiations on the Seven Rays. Can you not see that as President, you need to hold the overall vision? You cannot focus on one ray, you cannot focus on one area of society, you must look at the all. This, of course, is what can only happen when you have achieved some degree of Buddhic attainment where you have mastered the one requirement for Buddhic attainment: non-attachment.

Non-attachment to anything on earth so that when the demons of Mara come to knock on the door to the Oval Office, you are not tempted into reacting against what you see as a threat or acting in other ways that are unbalanced. Do you not see that when the demons of Mara came to tempt George Bush into reacting against the so-called terrorist threat, he was all too easily deceived into going to war in Iraq and

Afghanistan. Had it not been for the difficulties encountered in both places, he surely would have been deceived into taking down, or attempting to take down, the entire "Axis of Evil." For did he not, in fact, define his true goals when he gave that speech?

You cannot have a reactionary President

A good President cannot allow himself or herself to be pulled into this pattern of reacting *against* anything—or even reacting *for* anything in the material world. The President must be non-attached so that he can reach – or she can reach – for this higher vision that comes through the integration of the seven rays.

My beloved, you cannot achieve integration of the seven rays through the intellect or through the reasoning faculty. This is the deeper implication of what Lanto explained. You cannot achieve integration through the outer mind, through reason. No matter how well you know the characteristics of the seven rays, you still cannot integrate them. You can integrate them only through that total surrender whereby you come into oneness with the 8th Ray—and thus you *become* Integration.

You are not looking at the seven rays as being "out there" and you think that by somehow forcing them together, you have integrated them. Nay, for integration does not mean forcing together in the same space; it means allowing the individual rays to co-exist in their individual characteristics, but seeing those characteristics not as enemies or contradictory but as supplementing each other as the facets of the diamond. Thus, as President you must be able to look at the many different interest groups in this nation and not see them as being in opposition to each other, or as being mutually exclusive, but seeing past them and seeing the greater unity behind the individual expressions. Then, you serve as the open door for making the people see that greater unity as well, whereby they give up their animosities and are able to transcend their differences. Thus, they can also fathom the higher vision whereby they all become individual facets in the diamond that *is* the United States of America—or any other free and balanced nation. Thus, I Gautama, am grateful for this opportunity of anchoring this light here in America. I, Gautama Buddha, seal this series of releases. Thus, it is done! Gautama I AM.

20 | INVOKING A GOLDEN AGE PRESIDENT

In the name of the I AM THAT I AM, Jesus Christ, I use the authority that I have as a being in embodiment on earth to call upon Gautama Buddha to reinforce my calls and use my chakras to project the statements in this invocation into the collective consciousness and awaken Americans to their right to demand a golden age President. Awaken Americans to the reality that we are spiritual beings and that we can co-create a new future by working with the ascended masters. I especially call for …

[Make your own calls here.]

Part 1

1. By the authority of the Buddhic Flame in our hearts, we demand a President who realizes that as President of the United States, the only way to be successful is

to recognize that one cannot govern this nation out of one's own power.

> Gautama, show my mental state
> that does give rise to love and hate,
> your exposé I do endure,
> so my perception will be pure.
>
> **Gautama, Flame of Cosmic Peace,**
> **unruly thoughts do hereby cease,**
> **we radiate from you and me**
> **the peace to still Samsara's Sea.**

2. By the authority of the Buddhic Flame in our hearts, we demand a President who realizes that there must come that point of absolute and total surrender to a higher power, as one sees it.

> Gautama, in your Flame of Peace,
> the struggling self I now release,
> the Buddha Nature I now see,
> it is the core of you and me.
>
> **Gautama, Flame of Cosmic Peace,**
> **unruly thoughts do hereby cease,**
> **we radiate from you and me**
> **the peace to still Samsara's Sea.**

3. By the authority of the Buddhic Flame in our hearts, we demand a President who realizes that one needs to surrender the human ambition, the human expectations and the human pride that makes one think that one has the capacity to run this

20 | Invoking a Golden Age President

large and complex nation—a capacity that sets one above most other people.

> Gautama, I am one with thee,
> Mara's demons do now flee,
> your Presence like a soothing balm,
> my mind and senses ever calm.

> **Gautama, Flame of Cosmic Peace,**
> **unruly thoughts do hereby cease,**
> **we radiate from you and me**
> **the peace to still Samsara's Sea.**

4. By the authority of the Buddhic Flame in our hearts, we demand a President who realizes that once a President is sworn in, it is easy to believe in the lie that one is now the holder of the most powerful office in the world.

> Gautama, I now take the vow,
> to live in the eternal now,
> with you I do transcend all time,
> to live in present so sublime.

> **Gautama, Flame of Cosmic Peace,**
> **unruly thoughts do hereby cease,**
> **we radiate from you and me**
> **the peace to still Samsara's Sea.**

5. By the authority of the Buddhic Flame in our hearts, we demand a President who realizes that one might even think one is the most powerful person in the world, as many among the American people would like to think about their President.

Gautama, I have no desire,
to nothing earthly I aspire,
in non-attachment I now rest,
passing Mara's subtle test.

**Gautama, Flame of Cosmic Peace,
unruly thoughts do hereby cease,
we radiate from you and me
the peace to still Samsara's Sea.**

6. By the authority of the Buddhic Flame in our hearts, we demand a President who realizes that if one has personal pride, it is easy to believe in this. And if a person had no personal ambition, why would one even aspire to the office, given how conditions are with the political machinery in the United States.

Gautama, I melt into you,
my mind is one, no longer two,
immersed in your resplendent glow,
Nirvana is all that I know.

**Gautama, Flame of Cosmic Peace,
unruly thoughts do hereby cease,
we radiate from you and me
the peace to still Samsara's Sea.**

7. By the authority of the Buddhic Flame in our hearts, we demand a President who realizes that no one who has Buddhic attainment or Christ attainment would want to put himself or herself through the political machinery of the United States.

> Gautama, in your timeless space,
> I am immersed in Cosmic Grace,
> I know the God beyond all form,
> to world I will no more conform.
>
> **Gautama, Flame of Cosmic Peace,**
> **unruly thoughts do hereby cease,**
> **we radiate from you and me**
> **the peace to still Samsara's Sea.**

8. By the authority of the Buddhic Flame in our hearts, we demand a President who realizes that the people who are attracted to run for office – and who are willing to set aside their lives and give up their privacy forever – are those who have ambitions.

> Gautama, I am now awake,
> I clearly see what is at stake,
> and thus I claim my sacred right
> to be on earth the Buddhic Light.
>
> **Gautama, Flame of Cosmic Peace,**
> **unruly thoughts do hereby cease,**
> **we radiate from you and me**
> **the peace to still Samsara's Sea.**

9. By the authority of the Buddhic Flame in our hearts, we demand a President who realizes that this ambition comes from pride. For when one achieves the ambition, there will be a sense of pride, as is seen in almost every President. There are very few Presidents who have not had this pride.

Gautama, with your thunderbolt,
we give the earth a mighty jolt,
I know that some will understand,
and join the Buddha's timeless band.

**Gautama, Flame of Cosmic Peace,
unruly thoughts do hereby cease,
we radiate from you and me
the peace to still Samsara's Sea.**

Part 2

1. By the authority of the Buddhic Flame in our hearts, we demand a President who realizes that this pride is what makes a president think that he or she has the ability to govern. It is also what blocks the president from achieving total surrender.

Gautama, show my mental state
that does give rise to love and hate,
your exposé I do endure,
so my perception will be pure.

**Gautama, Flame of Cosmic Peace,
unruly thoughts do hereby cease,
we radiate from you and me
the peace to still Samsara's Sea.**

2. By the authority of the Buddhic Flame in our hearts, we demand a President who realizes that pride makes one unwilling to give up all human ambitions and expectations, and

simply say to the higher power: "Show me the way to go, show me how you would act in this situation."

Gautama, in your Flame of Peace,
the struggling self I now release,
the Buddha Nature I now see,
it is the core of you and me.

**Gautama, Flame of Cosmic Peace,
unruly thoughts do hereby cease,
we radiate from you and me
the peace to still Samsara's Sea.**

3. By the authority of the Buddhic Flame in our hearts, we demand a President who realizes that it is this inability or unwillingness to go through the total humility of complete surrender that is the reason the ascended masters are not anchoring a flame in the White House.

Gautama, I am one with thee,
Mara's demons do now flee,
your Presence like a soothing balm,
my mind and senses ever calm.

**Gautama, Flame of Cosmic Peace,
unruly thoughts do hereby cease,
we radiate from you and me
the peace to still Samsara's Sea.**

4. By the authority of the Buddhic Flame in our hearts, we demand a President who realizes that once the masters anchor a flame, all who pass through the flame will experience the

light. For some it will flush out their darkness, for others it will inspire and uplift them, but there will be an effect.

> Gautama, I now take the vow,
> to live in the eternal now,
> with you I do transcend all time,
> to live in present so sublime.
>
> **Gautama, Flame of Cosmic Peace,**
> **unruly thoughts do hereby cease,**
> **we radiate from you and me**
> **the peace to still Samsara's Sea.**

5. By the authority of the Buddhic Flame in our hearts, we demand a President who realizes that what the masters want for the White House is that as long as the President thinks he or she has the power to govern, then the president must be left alone so that he or she does not receive the light or the sponsorship from Above as an automatic grant.

> Gautama, I have no desire,
> to nothing earthly I aspire,
> in non-attachment I now rest,
> passing Mara's subtle test.
>
> **Gautama, Flame of Cosmic Peace,**
> **unruly thoughts do hereby cease,**
> **we radiate from you and me**
> **the peace to still Samsara's Sea.**

6. By the authority of the Buddhic Flame in our hearts, we demand a President who realizes that one receives it the

moment one humbles oneself, surrenders and asks for assistance from Above. Then, the assistance will be given in full measure.

> Gautama, I melt into you,
> my mind is one, no longer two,
> immersed in your resplendent glow,
> Nirvana is all that I know.

> **Gautama, Flame of Cosmic Peace,**
> **unruly thoughts do hereby cease,**
> **we radiate from you and me**
> **the peace to still Samsara's Sea.**

7. By the authority of the Buddhic Flame in our hearts, we demand a President who realizes that there will be a horizontal form of government until there is the willingness to reach up for that vertical assistance from Above; until there is a willingness to be the open door, the clear pane of glass, so that one can be "here below as Above."

> Gautama, in your timeless space,
> I am immersed in Cosmic Grace,
> I know the God beyond all form,
> to world I will no more conform.

> **Gautama, Flame of Cosmic Peace,**
> **unruly thoughts do hereby cease,**
> **we radiate from you and me**
> **the peace to still Samsara's Sea.**

8. By the authority of the Buddhic Flame in our hearts, we demand a President who realizes that another aspect of what

one need to achieve as President is practical realism. When one has the personal ambition, one also has a personal value judgment based on a relative dualistic standard. For one's ambition is to raise oneself to a certain status, and that can only be done according to a dualistic value judgment.

> Gautama, I am now awake,
> I clearly see what is at stake,
> and thus I claim my sacred right
> to be on earth the Buddhic Light.

> **Gautama, Flame of Cosmic Peace,**
> **unruly thoughts do hereby cease,**
> **we radiate from you and me**
> **the peace to still Samsara's Sea.**

9. By the authority of the Buddhic Flame in our hearts, we demand a President who realizes that when one has this pride, one is likely to be deceived into doing things that one thinks will be good according to one's personal ambition—which might be to leave a certain legacy.

> Gautama, with your thunderbolt,
> we give the earth a mighty jolt,
> I know that some will understand,
> and join the Buddha's timeless band.

> **Gautama, Flame of Cosmic Peace,**
> **unruly thoughts do hereby cease,**
> **we radiate from you and me**
> **the peace to still Samsara's Sea.**

Part 3

1. By the authority of the Buddhic Flame in our hearts, we demand a President who realizes that one is likely to be deceived into pursuing goals that are not realistic from a practical viewpoint, because they cannot be manifested, given the state of the collective consciousness and the practical situation that one faces as President.

> Gautama, show my mental state
> that does give rise to love and hate,
> your exposé I do endure,
> so my perception will be pure.

> **Gautama, Flame of Cosmic Peace,**
> **unruly thoughts do hereby cease,**
> **we radiate from you and me**
> **the peace to still Samsara's Sea.**

2. By the authority of the Buddhic Flame in our hearts, we demand a President who realizes that this is when one can become overly idealistic, wanting to hold on to the mental image and wanting, with all the power available to one as President, to force the nation, and even the world, to fit into one's mental box.

> Gautama, in your Flame of Peace,
> the struggling self I now release,
> the Buddha Nature I now see,
> it is the core of you and me.

**Gautama, Flame of Cosmic Peace,
unruly thoughts do hereby cease,
we radiate from you and me
the peace to still Samsara's Sea.**

3. By the authority of the Buddhic Flame in our hearts, we demand a President who realizes that pride can cause a President to lose the practical realism of what is the highest good for the highest number in the given situation. One will not acknowledge what the given situation truly is, for one wants the situation to live up to one's mental image.

Gautama, I am one with thee,
Mara's demons do now flee,
your Presence like a soothing balm,
my mind and senses ever calm.

**Gautama, Flame of Cosmic Peace,
unruly thoughts do hereby cease,
we radiate from you and me
the peace to still Samsara's Sea.**

4. By the authority of the Buddhic Flame in our hearts, we demand a President who realizes that there is no office that is more difficult to hold in the entire world than that of being President of the United States. It is because the United States has such a dominant position in the world.

Gautama, I now take the vow,
to live in the eternal now,
with you I do transcend all time,
to live in present so sublime.

**Gautama, Flame of Cosmic Peace,
unruly thoughts do hereby cease,
we radiate from you and me
the peace to still Samsara's Sea.**

5. By the authority of the Buddhic Flame in our hearts, we demand a President who realizes that America can be either the next empire that will attempt to take over the world, or it can be an example of a nation that will not be an empire, that will not have a king or an emperor.

> Gautama, I have no desire,
> to nothing earthly I aspire,
> in non-attachment I now rest,
> passing Mara's subtle test.

**Gautama, Flame of Cosmic Peace,
unruly thoughts do hereby cease,
we radiate from you and me
the peace to still Samsara's Sea.**

6. By the authority of the Buddhic Flame in our hearts, we demand a President who realizes that it was this example that George Washington set for the nation when he resigned his military commission and refused to run for a third term as President, refused to be President for Life. This is the example that must be upheld by the current President.

> Gautama, I melt into you,
> my mind is one, no longer two,
> immersed in your resplendent glow,
> Nirvana is all that I know.

**Gautama, Flame of Cosmic Peace,
unruly thoughts do hereby cease,
we radiate from you and me
the peace to still Samsara's Sea.**

7. By the authority of the Buddhic Flame in our hearts, we demand a President who realizes that it is absolutely necessary that this nation "under God" does not become an empire that pursues a human ambition, the ambition of the power elite who can never get enough power.

Gautama, in your timeless space,
I am immersed in Cosmic Grace,
I know the God beyond all form,
to world I will no more conform.

**Gautama, Flame of Cosmic Peace,
unruly thoughts do hereby cease,
we radiate from you and me
the peace to still Samsara's Sea.**

8. By the authority of the Buddhic Flame in our hearts, we demand a President who realizes that the power elite will continue to use the power available to them in a blind pursuit of their goals; their selfish, self-centered goals. The power elite have attempted to manipulate the United States behind the scenes and have attempted to secretly inflate the powers of the President.

Gautama, I am now awake,
I clearly see what is at stake,
and thus I claim my sacred right
to be on earth the Buddhic Light.

20 | Invoking a Golden Age President

**Gautama, Flame of Cosmic Peace,
unruly thoughts do hereby cease,
we radiate from you and me
the peace to still Samsara's Sea.**

9. By the authority of the Buddhic Flame in our hearts, we demand a President who realizes that the Office of the President has taken on far greater powers than is healthy or than was intended by the Founding Fathers.

Gautama, with your thunderbolt,
we give the earth a mighty jolt,
I know that some will understand,
and join the Buddha's timeless band.

**Gautama, Flame of Cosmic Peace,
unruly thoughts do hereby cease,
we radiate from you and me
the peace to still Samsara's Sea.**

Part 4

1. By the authority of the Buddhic Flame in our hearts, we demand a President who realizes that this was made even worse during the Bush presidency where the use of Executive Orders and Executive Powers went far beyond the intention of the Founding Fathers and what is good for the nation.

> Gautama, show my mental state
> that does give rise to love and hate,
> your exposé I do endure,
> so my perception will be pure.
>
> **Gautama, Flame of Cosmic Peace,**
> **unruly thoughts do hereby cease,**
> **we radiate from you and me**
> **the peace to still Samsara's Sea.**

2. By the authority of the Buddhic Flame in our hearts, we demand a President who realizes that the power elite have attempted to inflate the Office of the President because it is far easier to manipulate one President than to manipulate hundreds of Congressmen or a larger number of Supreme Court judges.

> Gautama, in your Flame of Peace,
> the struggling self I now release,
> the Buddha Nature I now see,
> it is the core of you and me.
>
> **Gautama, Flame of Cosmic Peace,**
> **unruly thoughts do hereby cease,**
> **we radiate from you and me**
> **the peace to still Samsara's Sea.**

3. By the authority of the Buddhic Flame in our hearts, we demand a President who realizes that when power is vested in just one person, that person is easily deceived by his or her personal ambition into making the wrong choices.

> Gautama, I am one with thee,
> Mara's demons do now flee,
> your Presence like a soothing balm,
> my mind and senses ever calm.
>
> **Gautama, Flame of Cosmic Peace,**
> **unruly thoughts do hereby cease,**
> **we radiate from you and me**
> **the peace to still Samsara's Sea.**

4. By the authority of the Buddhic Flame in our hearts, we demand a President who realizes that the power elite have set up a political machinery that is a sorting mechanism, sorting out those who are not willing to compromise in order to achieve their ambition.

> Gautama, I now take the vow,
> to live in the eternal now,
> with you I do transcend all time,
> to live in present so sublime.
>
> **Gautama, Flame of Cosmic Peace,**
> **unruly thoughts do hereby cease,**
> **we radiate from you and me**
> **the peace to still Samsara's Sea.**

5. By the authority of the Buddhic Flame in our hearts, we demand a President who realizes that the power elite have tried to make sure that anyone elected to the Office of President is willing to compromise in order to achieve his or her personal ambitions. The elite can manipulate that individual into making decisions in a crisis situation that are not good for the all.

Gautama, I have no desire,
to nothing earthly I aspire,
in non-attachment I now rest,
passing Mara's subtle test.

**Gautama, Flame of Cosmic Peace,
unruly thoughts do hereby cease,
we radiate from you and me
the peace to still Samsara's Sea.**

6. By the authority of the Buddhic Flame in our hearts, we demand a President who realizes that since George Washington's time the Office of the President has morphed into a position in the collective psyche that is different from what it was back then, where they often compared the President to a king or an emperor.

Gautama, I melt into you,
my mind is one, no longer two,
immersed in your resplendent glow,
Nirvana is all that I know.

**Gautama, Flame of Cosmic Peace,
unruly thoughts do hereby cease,
we radiate from you and me
the peace to still Samsara's Sea.**

7. By the authority of the Buddhic Flame in our hearts, we demand a President who realizes that now the Presidency has taken on a life of its own in the American psyche, and people now look to the President as an almost god-like figure whom they think has unlimited power.

Gautama, in your timeless space,
I am immersed in Cosmic Grace,
I know the God beyond all form,
to world I will no more conform.

**Gautama, Flame of Cosmic Peace,
unruly thoughts do hereby cease,
we radiate from you and me
the peace to still Samsara's Sea.**

8. By the authority of the Buddhic Flame in our hearts, we demand a President who realizes that the American people have been deceived into thinking that the President alone has greater powers than he actually has, even though he has greater powers than he should have in a more balanced political system.

Gautama, I am now awake,
I clearly see what is at stake,
and thus I claim my sacred right
to be on earth the Buddhic Light.

**Gautama, Flame of Cosmic Peace,
unruly thoughts do hereby cease,
we radiate from you and me
the peace to still Samsara's Sea.**

9. By the authority of the Buddhic Flame in our hearts, we demand a President who realizes that the people think the President can save them from their troubles, for they fail to realize that beyond the divisions of power set up by the Founding Fathers to limit the powers of the President, the greatest limiting power for the President is the collective consciousness.

> Gautama, with your thunderbolt,
> we give the earth a mighty jolt,
> I know that some will understand,
> and join the Buddha's timeless band.
>
> **Gautama, Flame of Cosmic Peace,
> unruly thoughts do hereby cease,
> we radiate from you and me
> the peace to still Samsara's Sea.**

Part 5

1. By the authority of the Buddhic Flame in our hearts, we demand a President who realizes that if America is to make the transition into the Golden Age, the political powers of the President need to be adjusted and the collective view of the President and the Office of the President need to go through a transformation so that people have a more realistic view.

> Gautama, show my mental state
> that does give rise to love and hate,
> your exposé I do endure,
> so my perception will be pure.
>
> **Gautama, Flame of Cosmic Peace,
> unruly thoughts do hereby cease,
> we radiate from you and me
> the peace to still Samsara's Sea.**

2. By the authority of the Buddhic Flame in our hearts, we demand a President who realizes that it is not enough for people

to go to the polls every four years and elect a new President. If people are not willing to transform their consciousness, to transcend their old mental boxes, it will make no difference that they elect a new President.

> Gautama, in your Flame of Peace,
> the struggling self I now release,
> the Buddha Nature I now see,
> it is the core of you and me.
>
> **Gautama, Flame of Cosmic Peace,**
> **unruly thoughts do hereby cease,**
> **we radiate from you and me**
> **the peace to still Samsara's Sea.**

3. By the authority of the Buddhic Flame in our hearts, we demand a President who realizes that it is necessary that the Office of the President is taken down in importance. For this to happen, it may be necessary that one or two presidents will suffer some humiliation so that the nation has an opportunity to learn.

> Gautama, I am one with thee,
> Mara's demons do now flee,
> your Presence like a soothing balm,
> my mind and senses ever calm.
>
> **Gautama, Flame of Cosmic Peace,**
> **unruly thoughts do hereby cease,**
> **we radiate from you and me**
> **the peace to still Samsara's Sea.**

4. By the authority of the Buddhic Flame in our hearts, we demand a President who realizes that the President is not God, but the President has the potential to be the open door for God—if he or she is willing to go through that total surrender and become a clear pane of glass.

> Gautama, I now take the vow,
> to live in the eternal now,
> with you I do transcend all time,
> to live in present so sublime.
>
> **Gautama, Flame of Cosmic Peace,**
> **unruly thoughts do hereby cease,**
> **we radiate from you and me**
> **the peace to still Samsara's Sea.**

5. By the authority of the Buddhic Flame in our hearts, we demand a President who realizes that one needs to hold the overall vision. One cannot focus on one area of society, one must look at the all. This can only happen when one has achieved some degree of non-attachment.

> Gautama, I have no desire,
> to nothing earthly I aspire,
> in non-attachment I now rest,
> passing Mara's subtle test.
>
> **Gautama, Flame of Cosmic Peace,**
> **unruly thoughts do hereby cease,**
> **we radiate from you and me**
> **the peace to still Samsara's Sea.**

6. By the authority of the Buddhic Flame in our hearts, we demand a President who realizes that a President must be non-attached to anything on earth, so that when the demons of Mara come to knock on the door to the Oval Office, one is not tempted into reacting against what one sees as a threat or acting in other ways that are unbalanced.

> Gautama, I melt into you,
> my mind is one, no longer two,
> immersed in your resplendent glow,
> Nirvana is all that I know.
>
> **Gautama, Flame of Cosmic Peace,**
> **unruly thoughts do hereby cease,**
> **we radiate from you and me**
> **the peace to still Samsara's Sea.**

7. By the authority of the Buddhic Flame in our hearts, we demand a President who realizes that a good President cannot allow himself or herself to be pulled into this pattern of reacting *against* anything—or even reacting *for* anything in the material world. The President must be non-attached so that he or she can reach for a higher vision.

> Gautama, in your timeless space,
> I am immersed in Cosmic Grace,
> I know the God beyond all form,
> to world I will no more conform.
>
> **Gautama, Flame of Cosmic Peace,**
> **unruly thoughts do hereby cease,**
> **we radiate from you and me**
> **the peace to still Samsara's Sea.**

8. By the authority of the Buddhic Flame in our hearts, we demand a President who realizes that one must be able to look at the many different interest groups in this nation and not see them as being in opposition to each other, or as being mutually exclusive, but seeing past them and seeing the greater unity behind the individual expressions. The President is then serving as the open door for making the people see that greater unity as well.

> Gautama, I am now awake,
> I clearly see what is at stake,
> and thus I claim my sacred right
> to be on earth the Buddhic Light.
>
> **Gautama, Flame of Cosmic Peace,**
> **unruly thoughts do hereby cease,**
> **we radiate from you and me**
> **the peace to still Samsara's Sea.**

9. By the authority of the Buddhic Flame in our hearts, we demand a President who realizes that when people give up their animosities and are able to transcend their differences, they can fathom the higher vision whereby they all become individual facets in the diamond that is the United States of America.

> Gautama, with your thunderbolt,
> we give the earth a mighty jolt,
> I know that some will understand,
> and join the Buddha's timeless band.

**Gautama, Flame of Cosmic Peace,
unruly thoughts do hereby cease,
we radiate from you and me
the peace to still Samsara's Sea.**

Sealing

In the name of the I AM THAT I AM, I accept that Archangel Michael, Astrea and Shiva form an impenetrable shield around myself and all constructive people, sealing us from all fear-based energies in all four octaves. I accept that the Light of God is consuming and transforming all fear-based energies that make up the dark forces working against America!

www.ingramcontent.com/pod-product-compliance
Lightning Source LLC
Chambersburg PA
CBHW030518230426
43665CB00010B/672